CHRISTOPHER REEVE

GREAT ACHIEVERS
LIVES OF THE PHYSICALLY CHALLENGED

CHRISTOPHER REEVE

ACTOR & ACTIVIST

Margaret L. Finn

Chelsea House Publishers

Philadelphia

FRONTIS: Even after his triumph in 1978's Superman *put him in great demand as an actor, Christopher Reeve still found time to support the causes he believed in. Here, he gets a hug from a Special Olympian in 1979.*

COVER PHOTOS: Reuters/Gary Hershorn/Archive Photos, AP Wide World Photos

CHELSEA HOUSE PUBLISHERS

EDITOR-IN-CHIEF Stephen Reginald
MANAGING EDITOR James D. Gallagher
PRODUCTION MANAGER Pamela Loos
ART DIRECTOR Sara Davis
PICTURE EDITOR Judy Hasday
SENIOR PRODUCTION EDITOR Lisa Chippendale

Staff for CHRISTOPHER REEVE
SENIOR EDITOR John Ziff
ASSOCIATE EDITOR Kristine Brennan
DESIGN AND TYPOGRAPHY Duke & Company
PICTURE RESEARCHER Sandy Jones
COVER DESIGN Keith Trego
COVER ILLUSTRATION Michael Garland

First Printing

1 3 5 7 9 8 6 4 2

Library of Congress Cataloging-in-Publication Data

Finn, Margaret L.
Christopher Reeve / Margaret L. Finn.
    p. cm.—(Great Achievers: lives of the physically challenged)
Includes bibliographical references and index.
Summary: A biography of the actor who found fame playing Superman in the movies and took on a new role as activist after becoming a quadriplegic.

ISBN 0-7910-4446-7 (hbk.)
        0-7910-4447-5 (pbk.)

1. Reeve, Christopher, 1952– —Juvenile literature. 2. Actors—United States—Biography—Juvenile literature. 3. Quadriplegics—United States—Biography—Juvenile literature. [1. Reeve, Christopher 1952–. 2. Actors. 3. Quadriplegics. 4. Physically handicapped.] I. Title. II. Series: Great achievers (Chelsea House Publishers)
PN2287.R292F56 1997
791.43′028′092—dc21   97-16605
[B]   CIP
                                                                                      AC

Excerpts from Mr. Reeve's 1996 Academy Awards ceremony speech appear courtesy of the Academy of Motion Picture Arts and Sciences, copyright © 1996.

CONTENTS

GREAT ACHIEVERS
LIVES OF THE PHYSICALLY CHALLENGED

A Message for Everyone

Jerry Lewis

Close to half a century ago—when I was the ripe old age of 23—an incredible stroke of fate rocketed me to overnight stardom as an entertainer. After the initial shock wore off, I began to have a very strong feeling that, in return for all life had given me, I must find a way of giving something back. At just that moment, a deeply moving experience in my personal life persuaded me to take up the leadership of a fledgling battle to defeat a then little-known group of diseases called muscular dystrophy, as well as other related neuromuscular diseases—all of which are disabling, and, in the worst cases, cut life short.

In 1950, when the Muscular Dystrophy Association (MDA)—of which I am national chairman—was established, physical disability was looked on as a matter of shame. Franklin Roosevelt, who guided America through World War II from a wheelchair, and Harold Russell, the World War II hero who lost both hands in battle, then became an Academy Award-winning movie star and chairman of the President's Committee on Employment of the Handicapped, were the exceptions. One of the reasons that muscular dystrophy and related diseases were so little known was that people who had been disabled by them were hidden at home, away from the pity and discomfort with which they were generally regarded by society. As I got to know and began working with people who have disabilities, I quickly learned what a tragic mistake this perception was. And my determination to correct this terrible problem soon became as great as my commitment to see disabling neuromuscular diseases wiped from the face of the earth.

I have long wondered why it never occurs to us, as we experience the knee-jerk inclination to feel sorry for people who are physically disabled, that lives such as those led by President Roosevelt, Harold Russell, and all of the extraordinary people profiled in this Great Achievers series demonstrate unmistakably how wrong we are. Physical disability need not be something that blights life and destroys opportunity for personal fulfillment and accomplishment. On the contrary, as people such as Ray Charles, Stephen Hawking, and Ron Kovic prove, physical disability can be a spur to greatness rather than a condemnation to emptiness.

In fact, if my experience with physically disabled people can be taken as a guide, as far as accomplishment is concerned, they have a slight edge on the rest of us. The unusual challenges they face require finding greater-than-average sources of energy and determination to achieve much of what able-bodied people take for granted. Often, this ultimately translates into a lifetime of superior performance in whatever endeavor people with disabilities choose to pursue.

If you have watched my Labor Day Telethon over the years, you know exactly what I am talking about. Annually, we introduce to tens of millions of Americans people whose accomplishments would distinguish them regardless of their physical conditions—top-ranking executives, physicians, scientists, lawyers, musicians, and artists. The message I hope the audience receives is not that these extraordinary individuals have achieved what they have by overcoming a dreadful disadvantage that the rest of us are lucky not to have to endure. Rather, I hope our viewers reflect on the fact that these outstanding people have been ennobled and strengthened by the tremendous challenges they have faced.

In 1992, MDA, which has grown over the past four decades into one of the world's leading voluntary health agencies, established a personal achievement awards program to demonstrate to the nation that the distinctive qualities of people with disabilities are by no means confined to the famous. What could have been more appropriate or timely in that year of the implementation of the 1990 Americans with Disabilities Act than to take an action that could perhaps finally achieve the alteration of public perception of disability, which MDA had struggled over four decades to achieve?

On Labor Day, 1992, it was my privilege to introduce to America MDA's inaugural national personal achievement award winner, Steve Mikita, assistant attorney general of the state of Utah. Steve graduated magna cum laude from Duke University as its first wheelchair student in history and was subsequently named the outstanding young lawyer of the year by the Utah Bar Association. After he spoke on the Telethon with an eloquence that caused phones to light up from coast to coast, people asked me where he had been all this time and why they had not known of him before, so deeply impressed were they by him. I answered that he and thousands like him have been here all along. We just have not adequately *noticed* them.

It is my fervent hope that we can eliminate indifference once and for all and make it possible for all of our fellow citizens with disabilities to gain their rightfully high place in our society.

ON FACING CHALLENGES

John Callahan

I was paralyzed for life in 1972, at the age of 21. A friend and I were driving in a Volkswagen on a hot July night, when he smashed the car at full speed into a utility pole. He suffered only minor injuries. But my spinal cord was severed during the crash, leaving me without any feeling from my diaphragm downward. The only muscles I could move were some in my upper body and arms, and I could also extend my fingers. After spending a lot of time in physical therapy, it became possible for me to grasp a pen.

I've always loved to draw. When I was a kid, I made pictures of everything from Daffy Duck (one of my lifelong role models) to caricatures of my teachers and friends. I've always been a people watcher, it seems; and I've always looked at the world in a sort of skewed way. Everything I see just happens to translate immediately into humor. And so, humor has become my way of coping. As the years have gone by, I have developed a tremendous drive to express my humor by drawing cartoons.

The key to cartooning is to put a different spin on the expected, the normal. And that's one reason why many of my cartoons deal with the disabled: amputees, quadriplegics, paraplegics, and the blind. The public is not used to seeing them in cartoons.

But there's another reason why my subjects are often disabled men and women. I'm sick and tired of people who presume to speak for the disabled. Call me a cripple, call me a gimp, call me paralyzed for life.

Just don't call me something I'm not. I'm not "differently abled," and my cartoons show that disabled people should not be treated any differently than anyone else.

All of the men, women, and children who are profiled in the Great Achievers series share this in common: their various handicaps have not prevented them from accomplishing great things. Their life stories are worth knowing about because they have found the strength and courage to develop their talents and to follow their dreams as fully as they can.

Whether able-bodied or disabled, a person must strive to overcome obstacles. There's nothing greater than to see a person who faces challenges and conquers them, regardless of his or her limitations.

Reeve's surprise appearance at the 68th Academy Awards ceremony was greeted with jubilation by the crowd assembled at the Dorothy Chandler Pavilion—and by a spellbound television audience—on March 25, 1996.

1

HOLLYWOOD'S CONSCIENCE

There's no challenge, artistic or otherwise, that we can't meet.
—Christopher Reeve, 68th Academy Awards ceremony

THE VAST BLUE stage of the Dorothy Chandler Pavilion in Los Angeles stood empty—except for a lone man—in the midst of the festive 68th Academy Awards ceremonies on the night of March 25, 1996. He sat stiffly propped in a wheelchair at center stage before a monumental backdrop of four white pilasters against a field of blue. Just before the red and gold curtain had been raised to reveal him, a hush had enveloped the theater—an abrupt departure from the dizzying spectacle of lavish sets, musicians, and breathless award winners that had unfolded so far.

An immediate spark of recognition detonated an explosion of applause from the crowd, as all stood to honor a colleague and leader who was making a surprise appearance.

From his wheelchair, Christopher Reeve—wearing a tuxedo and strikingly handsome at 43, with strong, angular features and flashing blue eyes—scanned the crowd nervously at first, his face taut, his eyes wide, then broke into a boyish grin. His head supported by a brace attached to the chair, his hands lying limp on concave black leather rests, his legs and feet immobile against their supports, he waited for the thunderous applause to subside. His left eyebrow arched as his eyes widened and his smile broadened with a fierce thrill of pride and of joy.

A clear round plastic tube lay across his chest where a tie might have hung. It ended in a metal junction at a white bandage across his throat, filling the center of his open white shirt collar like an ascot. What the crowd applauding him and almost a billion television viewers around the world could not see was a rectangular metal box behind him: a respirator sitting between the two rear wheels of the chair. It was the source of the plastic tube—and of the air that was keeping him alive.

Reeve—who had soared to fame playing the role of Superman in the blockbuster 1978 movie—had shattered his first and second vertebrae and damaged part of his spinal cord when his horse stalled at a jump during a competition in Culpeper County, Virginia, on May 27, 1995. Forward momentum had carried the athletic six-foot, four-inch actor over the jump to strike the ground headfirst, rendering him paralyzed from the neck down.

Buoyed by the love of his wife, Dana, he had resolved to survive—and to thrive.

Onstage at the Dorothy Chandler Pavilion less than a year after his accident, Reeve scanned the audience that still stood applauding him: he saw a sea of bejeweled women in evening gowns and men in tuxedos.

Whistles and whoops of joy punctuated the applause, as Reeve smiled and said, "Thank you," in a barely audible voice. Film giants who had collected Oscars throughout the years—Tom Hanks (for *Philadelphia* and *Forrest Gump*) and Meryl Streep (for *Sophie's Choice* and *Kramer vs. Kramer*) —smiled and applauded their colleague. Mel Gibson, who would take the Oscars for best picture and best director for *Braveheart* that night, held his hands high to applaud a man who, like him, had performed his own stunts in high-action films. "Thank you very much," Reeve murmured, smiling.

Months of frustrating rehabilitation had followed his tragic

fall. He relentlessly worked useless muscles that had once propelled him through his favorite sports: skiing, sailing, tennis, biking, scuba diving, soccer, and hiking. Inured to his immobile existence, Reeve had fought hard to make gradual improvements, to breathe without a respirator, to speak with ease. He had begun to make his way out into the world again. In January he had received an invitation from the Academy of Motion Picture Arts and Sciences to appear on the awards show in March. Determination, a hallmark of Reeve's character, prompted him to accept.

The road to the Dorothy Chandler Pavilion stage proved arduous. Two months of painstaking preparation paved the way. By March, a group of specialists—including Neil Stutzer, president of Access of New Jersey, an organization that facilitates travel for the disabled—had joined Academy board members to examine the Dorothy Chandler Pavilion layout and to devise security and travel plans for the jour-

The crowd reacts to Reeve's appearance at the Academy Awards. After the applause subsided, Reeve made a presentation urging motion picture artists to continue tackling social issues on film.

ney from Reeve's Westchester, New York, home. Stutzer's 75-page manual even prepared the team for the eventuality of Reeve's wheelchair needing repair. Warner Bros. provided a jet to fly Reeve and his wife to Los Angeles at the request of Academy Awards show producer Quincy Jones.

Reeve and his entourage of doctors and attendants arrived in Los Angeles on March 23. Not wanting to be recognized, he checked into the Beverly Hilton using an assumed name and made his way to the presidential suite through hallways cleared by hotel security officers. On Oscar day, a specially equipped van whisked him to the pavilion for rehearsals and returned him for the 6:00 P.M. show, which was to air at 9:00 P.M. eastern standard time.

Throughout the preparations for Oscar night, Reeve worried that he would be powerless to prevent violent arm and leg spasms once he got onstage before the huge audience. Spotlights could cause dangerous overheating, since Reeve's brain could no longer instruct his body to perspire, but he was determined to avoid mishaps and embarrassment.

Disaster threatened for a moment, however, when Reeve rolled out of his dressing room. His chair hit a bump. He fell forward from the waist, his arms and legs dangling. But his aides quickly righted him in his chair.

Onstage, as the applause subsided and eager well-wishers sat down, Reeve grew serious and fixed his gaze on the television camera. He smiled apprehensively and waited for the respirator to fill his chest with air.

"What you probably don't know is that I left New York last September, and I just arrived here this morning," he joked in a quiet voice. Laughter rippled across the audience. "And I'm glad I did," he added, biting his lip, "because I wouldn't have missed this kind of welcome for the world. Thank you." His eyes shone.

His arms and legs did not suffer spasms. "I sort of willed myself not to have anything go wrong," he later told a reporter. He was to be an announcer like any other in the show that night. His job was to present a special segment of the show, a selection of highlights taken from films dealing with social issues.

From the moment of his entrance, Reeve's performance became one with its own social message. He spoke quickly, a few sentences at a time, his words dying as he ran out of breath; then he waited for the respirator to supply him with enough air to speak again. "When I was a kid," he began, "my friends and I went to the movies just for fun. . . ." Again, a pause until his lungs refilled with air. Eleven times per minute, the respirator inflated his lungs, causing his chest to rise visibly. "But then we saw [Stanley] Kubrick's *Dr. Strangelove;* it started us thinking about the madness of nuclear destruction." Reeve paused again. His extraordinary effort to communicate demonstrated both the horror of his incapacity and the power of his will to surmount it. He became an example for all who struggle to overcome hardship of any kind.

He said that director Stanley Kramer's *The Defiant Ones* had taught him about race relations. "We began to realize that films could deal with social issues," he said. "Now when you look at films like *Platoon* [about Vietnam] and *Philadelphia* [about AIDS], you realize the power of film to present painful and important issues to the public." He went on to introduce a montage of clips from films that "have courageously put social issues ahead of box office success." Among the 11 films featured were 1991's *Thelma and Louise,* which addressed the plight of a rape victim in a male-dominated society; *In the Heat of the Night,* which took on racial bigotry when it was released in 1967; *Coming Home,* which, in 1978, told the tale of a paraplegic Vietnam vet turning against the war; and 1979's *Norma Rae,* which championed the plight of small-town factory workers seeking to unionize for fair wages. The poignant strains of Barber's "Adagio for Strings" accompanied an aerial shot of bodies dotting a bomb crater in *Platoon,* a film made in 1986, when the nation was ready to take a very graphic look back at the Vietnam War. Finally, Liam Neeson, playing the title character from 1993's

Reeve credits his wife Dana with restoring his will to live in the days following his accident. Buoyed by her love, he has resumed an active life as a fund-raiser and advocate for the disabled.

Schindler's List, spoke tearfully of the many Jews whom he had been unable to save from Nazi death camps. "I didn't do enough," Neeson said. "I should have done more."

"Hollywood needs to do more," Reeve said, as the screen darkened. "Let's continue to take risks. Let's tackle the issues in many ways. In many ways our film community can do it better than anyone else. There is no challenge, artistic or otherwise, that we can't meet." Running out of air, he softly said, "Thank you."

Reeve had been preparing for the role of humanitarian activist throughout his career. He cofounded the Creative Coalition, an organization of actors and actresses that has raised public awareness of social issues. He has also actively fought to protect the environment and endangered animal species, and he has helped Save the Children, Amnesty International, and other social welfare groups.

Now a quadriplegic, Reeve crusades for the rights of those

like him. He has lobbied in Washington for an increase in federal funding for spinal-cord injury (SCI) research and for greater insurance coverage for SCI and brain damage victims. Reeve has set a goal of standing on his own by the time he turns 50. Whether he achieves that goal or not, his example has given others the message that, with determination and support, almost anything is possible. As a role model and an activist, he stands taller today than ever before.

Steve McQueen is a prisoner of war who slips away from his German captors in The Great Escape. *This 1963 adventure film prompted young Christopher Reeve and his friends to reenact McQueen's daring ride on their bicycles.*

2

FINDING A CIVILIZATION, 1952–74

"That's it. That's it," Pig agreed enthusiastically. "This is a family.
We got two thousand brothers who will [be there] for any one of us."
—Pat Conroy, *The Lords of Discipline*

CHRISTOPHER REEVE TOOK his first breath on September 25, 1952, in New York City. His parents, Barbara and Franklin d'Olier Reeve, lived in an apartment on East 88th Street, not far from Columbia University, where Franklin (now known as F. D. Reeve), novelist, poet, and Russian literature scholar, was working to earn a Ph.D.—and struggling to make ends meet. Between classes and research he waited tables, hauled freight as a longshoreman, performed in political activist theater, and taught Slavic languages at Columbia.

Young Franklin had chosen the hard way to success. A child of privilege, born in 1928 in Philadelphia and reared in an upscale section of Morristown, New Jersey, Franklin broke with his family in the 1940s. His ancestors had held a distinguished place in history for many centuries. One served as an ambassador to Constantinople for Louis XIV, "the Sun King," who ruled France from 1643 to 1715. Other d'Olier ancestors, French nobles, held titles. Franklin's great-grandfather, Michel, born in Montauben, France, grew up in County Mayo, Ireland, and married there. Michel's son, William, came to the United States and founded

Reeve's great-grandfather Franklin d'Olier (right) was one of his many accomplished ancestors. D'Olier is shown here with Colonel Frederick W. Galbraith sometime after ending his tenure as commander of the American Legion.

several cotton mills in Philadelphia in 1869, laying the foundation for the family's wealth. In 1919, Christopher's great-grandfather, Colonel Franklin d'Olier, cofounded the American Legion, a patriotic service organization of war veterans, with 19 other officers, including Theodore Roosevelt, who had been president of the United States from 1901 to 1909. Colonel d'Olier served as the Legion's first national commander. Later, as a pilot in the aftermath of World War II, he flew over major Japanese cities to assess the damage done by American bombing. He also served as president of the Prudential Insurance Company from 1938 to 1946.

Christopher's father entered Princeton University in 1946 and graduated in 1950 with a bachelor of arts degree in English. He married Barbara Pitney Lamb, a distant relative,

while she was an undergraduate at Vassar College in Pough-keepsie, New York. At Columbia, Reeve would go on to an associate professorship in Russian literature.

Barbara was still a teenager when she gave birth to blond, blue-eyed Christopher in 1952. Franklin chose his friend Frank Kermode, biographer of British novelist D. H. Lawrence, to be Christopher's godfather. A year later, Barbara —still not yet 20—gave birth to another son, Benjamin, who would one day become a writer and a lawyer.

Young Reeve's idyllic toddler years of carriage rides through Central Park, tumbling about the apartment with Ben, and listening to bedtime tales was turned upside down in his fourth year, when Barbara and Franklin's marriage shattered. On December 31, 1956, Barbara took Christopher

Reeve's mother, Barbara Johnson. Despite the turmoil he experienced when his parents divorced, Reeve attributes his love of learning and the arts to the encouragement he received from both his mother and his father, F. D. Reeve.

and Benjamin with her to Princeton, and the bitterness between Franklin and Barbara sundered Christopher's halcyon family life.

American novelist Pat Conroy wrote in *The Lords of Discipline,* the harrowing story of his years in military school, that with every divorce, a civilization is destroyed. Four-year-old Reeve's own civilization—his haven of safety and system of shared traditions—collapsed at a time when he was too young to understand what was happening.

As time went by, the divorced parents vied for the boys' affections. "I felt torn between them," he told writer Sarah Matthiessen in 1980. "They had a tendency to use me as a chess piece."

In time, both parents would remarry. F. D. Reeve left Columbia to teach writing and poetry at the University of Illinois, then at Yale, and finally at Wesleyan University in Connecticut, where he teaches today. In June 1959, when Christopher was seven, Barbara married wealthy investment banker Tristan Johnson, who already had four children from an earlier marriage. Barbara wrote for the Princeton local news weekly, *Town Topics.* She eventually gave birth to two more children with Johnson. F. D. Reeve and his new wife had three children of their own, so Christopher struggled to find his own place among his one full, four step-, and five half-siblings. He had become 1 of 11 children.

"It was all just bits and pieces," he told biographer Roger Rosenblatt many years later. "You just [didn't] want to risk getting involved with people for fear that things [were] going to fall apart."

Tristan Johnson, although strict, was, in Reeve's own words, a "kind and generous father" at their Campleton Circle home in Princeton. While he forbade television watching and comic book reading and encouraged study and more active pursuits, he provided an education for Reeve at the exclusive Princeton Day School. Reeve later complained to one writer about having been deprived of comic books, but he would tell another that his upbringing was "very privileged."

Princeton afforded Reeve an environment that differed vastly from most. Princeton proper, less than two square miles in area, centers on Princeton University, an Ivy League school with a proud history. The 19th-century Gothic spires and ivy-covered buildings of the university, its students and professors dressed in tweeds and argyle sweaters, and the quaint, upscale shops throughout the small town formed the familiar landscape of his youth.

Reeve was well acquainted with Princeton's history of attracting famous intellectuals: Albert Einstein, who developed the theory of relativity, lived in Princeton from 1936 to 1955, and Presidents Woodrow Wilson and Grover Cleveland made their homes in the university town.

A sense of intellectual and cultural camaraderie also existed among the general populace of Princeton. When he was six, Reeve's mother took him every Sunday to the Princeton Society of Musical Amateurs. "They would gather and read a major chorale work with a full symphony orchestra, a 95-piece orchestra composed of housewives and plumbers, anybody who could play a musical instrument," he recalled. "At six years old, I was sitting there in the soprano section with my mother. . . . I'm very grateful that I had that."

At age six Reeve also began to spend weekends learning to ski in the Pocono Mountains of Pennsylvania with his family. Sports became a passion for him. He excelled at tennis, and, at school, he competed in fencing and varsity hockey.

One interviewer later asked him if his "enormous willpower" stemmed from being so athletic. "I think so," he responded. "As a kid, I was always competitive, and I've always responded well to a challenge. If someone says, 'You've got to try 20 repetitions of this exercise.' that gives me an incentive to do 30 or 35. You have to push."

Winning became so important to Reeve that when a teacher recommended that he skip a grade at age eight, a school psychologist advised against it because, while he was smart enough to make the leap, it was feared that he would force himself to the top of the class—too much stress for an eight-year-old.

Reeve spent much of his time in solitary pursuits like playing the piano and swimming competitively. But he also enjoyed social activities, like going to movies with friends. He and his friends especially liked *The Great Escape,* in which American and British soldiers plot to escape a German prison camp in 1944. Reeve and his friends thrilled at the spectacle of Steve McQueen zooming across the German countryside on a motorcycle in a daredevil attempt to escape from Nazis in hot pursuit. He and his friends, like boys across the country, spent endless hours imitating McQueen on their bicycles. "I was about 11 when [the movie] came out," he told writer Michael Hill. "It really, really grabbed me." In their teens, Reeve and his friends found not only adventure at the movies, but a world far beyond their idyllic life in the cultured but insular town of Princeton.

Reeve grew up in close proximity to some of the great American minds of his time. His own father was among them. In 1962 the senior Reeve traveled to Russia as a translator for the renowned American poet Robert Frost and wrote the book *Robert Frost in Russia* that year; *The Russian Novel* followed in 1964. Since then, F. D. Reeve has written many books of poetry and a history of the Russian symbolist movement, *Between Image and Idea.* He has translated and edited a collection of five novels by 19th-century Russian author Ivan Turgenev, as well as many critical articles on 19th- and 20th-century Russian novelists. He has also written several novels.

While visiting his father, who taught at Yale University in New Haven, Connecticut, Reeve would join in discussions with his father's friends: poets Robert Frost and Robert Penn Warren and sociologist Daniel Moynihan, who later became a U.S. senator from New York. This was heady company for a boy of Reeve's age.

During his weekends in New Haven, Reeve learned from his father how to sail, eventually racing his father's sailboat.

True to his nature, he won most of his races, but he would subject his crew to his own high standards, aggressively pushing them to their limits, what he later called "terror[izing]" them.

Despite all the benefits of wealth and privilege, Reeve was still a boy affected by his parents' divorce and by the shuttling between households he and Benjamin endured for 15 years while neither parent spoke to the other. He found it difficult to adjust to two different "civilizations," neither of which was entirely his own. However, he soon found a new world far away from his family strife.

When he was in the fourth grade, a representative of Princeton's famous McCarter Theatre came into his science

The Princeton University campus, seen through an archway. Princeton afforded Christopher Reeve an environment that was both sheltered and richly peopled with academics, statesmen, and a general populace that valued the arts and cultural pursuits.

class to ask if anyone could sing. "I sang, 'mi, mi, mi,'" he told an interviewer. With that, he was cast in a soprano singing role in Gilbert and Sullivan's *The Yeoman of the Guard.* So began his love affair with acting.

Reeve eagerly sought and won almost every lead role in every play or musical at the Princeton Day School. He also continued to perform with the McCarter Theatre on a regular basis, first in child roles in *The Diary of Anne Frank,* the true story of a young girl hiding with her family from Hitler's death squads, and in Thornton Wilder's *Our Town,* a tale of love, life, and death in a rural American town. In time he came to play adult parts in McCarter Theatre productions, including Sean O'Casey's *The Plough and the Stars,* a play about the Irish revolution. He would later recall that instead of feeling like a chess piece caught between his parents, he felt safe in the theater.

Aside from the literary influence of F. D. Reeve, there was Princeton itself to steer Christopher toward a career in fine arts. "I think living in Princeton with that kind of academic and musical sophistication that town has was very important to my acting," he told writer Barbara Kantrowitz in 1981. "I think if I had grown up in East Orange [New Jersey] or some place like that I might have done something else. Not to dump on East Orange. But I didn't have to be led to water. I was already there. I was already in the pool, so to speak."

Reeve also credited his parents' encouragement. "What my parents did was to make musical discovery and academic discovery fun," he recalled as an adult.

In the theater, Reeve found other mentors, including John Lithgow (*The World According to Garp, Third Rock from the Sun*), the son of the McCarter Theatre's owners. Like his friend Reeve, Lithgow is renowned for his fine stage, television, and film work.

By the time he reached his early teens, Reeve found another reason to love the stage. "I can remember that [the theater] solved the problem of Friday and Saturday nights," he later recalled. "I didn't have to worry about how I was going to ask little Suzy out for a date, because I was too busy in the theater anyway." He added, "I would think if I'm really lucky she'll come to see the play, think I'm terrific, [and] then I'll have a better chance."

Reeve had good reason for his teenage insecurity. Six feet, two inches tall at age 14, he towered over his classmates. He suffered from Osgood-Schlatter's disease, which prevents tendons in the legs from keeping up with the rate of bone growth. "As a result I was very awkward. And enormous," he remembered. "And I moved like a building. Even though I was attractive, I lacked self-confidence. The theater was a nice place to go solve those problems."

By now Reeve's parents had come to realize that acting would be his career, and they supported him in achieving his goal. He studied stagecraft and makeup at the Lawrence-ville School, near Princeton, during the summer between 9th and 10th grades. The following summer he began a lifelong relationship with the famous Williamstown Theatre in Massa-chusetts by serving as an apprentice. In his 16th summer he performed at the Loeb Drama Center in Cambridge, Mas-sachusetts, as Beliaev, a principal character in Turgenev's *A Month in the Country.* He also performed in *Death of a Sales-man, The Hostage,* and *The Threepenny Opera* at Loeb. That year he also appeared in Maine's Boothbay Playhouse pro-duction of *Private Lives* and in the San Diego Shakespeare Festival's production of *Troilus and Cressida.*

He was still only 16 when he joined Actors' Equity Asso-ciation and found an agent. Straight out of high school he joined the touring company of *The Irregular Verb to Love,* starring opposite well-known actress Celeste Holm. His sum-mer venture to learn the craft of theater between 9th and 10th grades had blossomed into a full-fledged professional act-ing career just three summers later.

That fall, in 1970, Reeve left Princeton for Ithaca, New York, to attend Cornell University. It was a time of unrest on college campuses across the country. Students protesting the Vietnam War boycotted classes, occupied college and university administration buildings, and flocked to massive demonstrations in Washington, D.C., to urge President Richard Nixon to withdraw American forces. Many college students abandoned traditional dress, donned bellbottomed blue jeans, grew their hair long and straight—and formed a collective counterculture. It was the era of Woodstock, of songs pleading, "Give peace a chance," and of hippies touting "flower power."

Reeve later said, "I didn't get into actual activism in the sense of taking over buildings. . . . I remember things like Earth Day and, of course, Woodstock, and I remember very well the protest against the invasion of Cambodia and campaigning for [liberal Democratic presidential candidate George] McGovern."

What Christopher Reeve *did* do in college was act.

"I used to come down from Cornell, cut classes for a day, and make appointments for films and TV," he told an interviewer. "And then I'd go back and make up the homework. So I did the occasional television spot while I was still at college." In his free time he took advantage of the nearby ski resorts.

Reeve continued to perform at regional summer theaters. He also took an apprenticeship at the famed Old Vic in London, observing backstage, and he apprenticed at the equally renowned Comédie Française in Paris.

By his senior year, Reeve had amassed such an impressive list of professional performances that the prestigious Juilliard School in New York—which in 1968 had added drama instruction to its highly rated music educational program—admitted him and only two other students to its advanced drama program. "I did everything at Juilliard," he later told an interviewer, "voice work, some ballet, fencing, stage fighting, acrobatics, circus, mime—all of it."

Reeve remained in New York City at Juilliard for a year after graduating Cornell in 1974 with a bachelor of arts degree. There, as his father had, he ventured out to find work to support himself and to pay his tuition. He was now 21 and no longer an awkward teenager. His straight brown hair framed a handsome face with high cheekbones and a square jaw; his eyes flashed a startlingly clear aqua blue, and his smile creased into dimples, revealing straight white teeth. With his leading-man looks, Reeve was about to find more than he bargained for in his "part-time" job.

In his twenties Reeve was a far cry from the awkward teenager who had found a refuge from his insecurities in the theater. His good looks would help propel him from rakish soap-opera character to movie superhero.

3

IT TAKES A PILOT
TO FLY, 1974–78

You must see on a man's face a certain delight,
a certain joy in flying that can only come out of inner conviction.
—Christopher Reeve

WHEN REEVE LANDED the part of tennis bum Ben Harper—a cold-hearted bigamist in the daytime television soap opera *Love of Life*—to finance his second year at Juilliard, he had no idea that the role would "do so well," he told one writer several years later. Excelling in his first television role brought Reeve national fame among daytime television viewers, but with it came an increasingly impossible schedule as he tried to balance school with work. His original one- or two-day stint at the CBS studios now consumed most of his week.

He considered the advice of one of his instructors at Juilliard, the esteemed stage actor and director John Houseman, who said, "Mr. Reeve, it's very important that you become a serious actor. Unless of course, they offer you a load of money to do something else." Reeve left school to act full-time both in television and on the stage.

At Juilliard he had made a new friend, Robin Williams, who would one day soar to fame on television with the hit series *Mork and Mindy*, and on film with *Mrs. Doubtfire, The Birdcage,* and many more. So opposite in their acting styles—Williams, lighthearted and zany, and

Reeve, intensely serious—the two had formed a sustaining, lifelong friendship.

Reeve, despite his disapproval of the shallow soap opera scripts, nevertheless plunged heartily into his role as Ben Harper, "if only for the challenge of making something out of bad material," he told author Adrian Havill. "In college you perform the masterpieces, the classics. It isn't like that in real life."

But Reeve also performed more serious roles with the Circle Repertory Company and the Manhattan Theater Club while he was starring in *Love of Life.* Then, in 1975, he landed his first Broadway role, in Enid Bagnold's *A Matter of Gravity,* playing Nicky, grandson of Mrs. Basil, who was played by screen and stage star Katharine Hepburn. The play, about

Although the earnest Christopher Reeve and the irreverent Robin Williams (right) may appear to have little in common, the two enjoy a lifelong friendship that began when both were drama students at Juilliard.

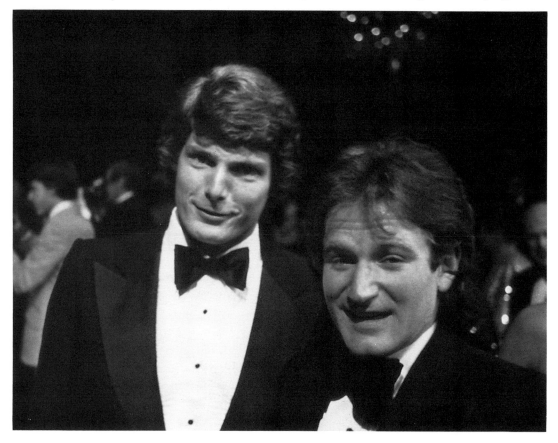

age and loss, takes place in the antique-filled drawing room of Mrs. Basil's decaying manor house. Nicky, an Oxford student, has brought his homosexual and politically strident friends to visit his grandmother, who seizes upon the occasion to criticize the younger generation and its socialist bent. At one point she says, "You are sucking up to the common man's age, and, my word, it's common!"

Hepburn, noted for her class, wit, and sagacity, took Reeve under her wing during the play's rehearsals. "She used to say to me, 'Now be fascinating, Reeve, now be fascinating!'" he told *Newsweek* writer Jack Kroll in 1979. "Well that's easy for you to say," he would respond. "The rest of us have to work at it, you know." Reeve did gain what he later called his "best unconscious acting lesson" from Hepburn. "I'd always thought of acting as a way to lose yourself, disappear into a part and thus find a kind of freedom. She taught me that quite the opposite is supposed to happen. You must bring your own convictions, things you really love and hate, to the character and then adjust after that."

After several weeks of tryouts in Philadelphia and Washington, D.C., the play opened in New York on February 3, 1976, to tepid reviews. Brendan Gill of *The New Yorker* considered it merely a "vehicle" for Hepburn, and *Newsweek*'s Charles Michener called it "a comedy of bad manners." Reeve was said by one critic to have "done justice to a role that required only his presence." He reflected on the play several years later: ". . . [P]eople say to me, 'Oh . . . you're playing the leading man opposite Katharine Hepburn! My God! What a success!' But the play wasn't very good, the production was weak, and it wasn't a success in my terms, because [it] didn't come alive until its second tour. Just to be someplace is not a success. It's what you make of it."

Balancing television and stage roles, Reeve had become far too thin, looking gaunt and lanky. "I was down to 180 pounds and was absolutely a wreck," he recalled. "I looked ashen . . . really bad, because I was riding the rails between Toronto or Washington . . . and I would have to get out at

Although he performed in the classics at Juilliard, Reeve relished his experience playing Ben Harper on Love of Life *because it increased his mastery of ensemble acting. Here Reeve enjoys a reunion with the cast and crew of* Love of Life *after finding fame as Superman.*

4:00 in the morning to take a plane to New York, learning the lines on the plane since I had to be at CBS by 7:30 to do a full day's work on the soap till 5:00 in the evening. Then I'd hop another plane at 6:00, shuttle back to Washington or wherever and be on stage at 8:00. That was twice a week for 16 weeks."

While still performing in *A Matter of Gravity,* Reeve got a call that would change his life. It was Lynn Stalmaster, one of Hollywood's top casting agents. Ilya Salkind was producing a new movie with his father, Alexander, about the comic-strip hero Superman. He was seeking a young actor to play the lead role. No major star who was available was right for the part, so they had decided to look for an unknown actor who actually looked like the square-jawed, athletic superhero. Ilya had found Reeve's picture in the *Academy Players Directory.* Would he come to London to interview with director Richard Donner?

"I thought I was a ridiculous [choice] for Superman, weighing about 180 pounds," Reeve told author David Michael Petrou. "But I always take a reading whatever it is even if it's the lead role in *The Joy of Cooking* [a popular cookbook]." Reeve had reservations about the role, though. "At first I thought . . . who needs this?" he said. "This is going to be a multi-million dollar disaster . . . this is *King Kong*!" But, true to his credo, he went.

Reeve arrived at Shepperton Studios, outside of London, looking "drawn and perhaps a little too lanky," according to Stalmaster. He, Ilya Salkind, and Richard Donner talked for a long time about everything but *Superman*; Donner was not impressed. The young Reeve, although obviously handsome, intelligent, and talented, was too young and too skinny, and not famous enough to be a box-office draw. Salkind expressed enthusiasm though, especially when they talked Reeve into putting on a pair of horn-rimmed glasses and pretending to be Clark Kent, Superman's awkward, insecure alter ego. Without accord, though, they let him go.

Realizing he hadn't landed the part, Reeve returned to New York and continued with *A Matter of Gravity* until it closed in April 1976. That month, he headed out to California and landed his first screen role, a small part in a submarine disaster movie by Universal called *Gray Lady Down,* which starred Charlton Heston. Critics panned the film (one called it "a disaster about a disaster"), and Reeve spent the next five months floundering. "I absolutely wrote myself off," he said. "I was sponging off friends, sleeping on couches, turning into a vegetable, and then one day I said, 'This isn't right.'" He returned to New York and found a starring role as a grandfather reflecting on his life in the off-Broadway play *Kite Flying,* by Corinne Jacker. Reviews were mixed.

By late January 1977, in London, the Salkinds and Donner, having failed to find a superstar—or anybody—who really looked like Superman, were running out of time. It was a month and five days before filming was to start. Out of 200 choices, from superstars to beachcombers—even one dentist—they had narrowed the field to 20 actors. Donner and associate producer Pierre Spengler still considered Reeve too young, but since they had options to make up to six sequels, they conceded that a young actor might be right for the part. They sent him a copy of the script and invited him to take a screen test. Reading it laid to rest Reeve's doubts about the seriousness of the project. "I . . . found it *was* an intelligent new script," he told an interviewer. Finding that the producers had signed on major stars like Marlon Brando (for $3.7 million), Gene Hackman (for $2 million), Trevor Howard, and Terence Stamp to play key roles, he realized that the Salkinds' *Superman* was "no joke."

Reeve came prepared for the screen test. According to Ilya Salkind, his characterization of Clark Kent—complete with gray flannel suit, black wing-tip shoes, gloves, and slicked-down hair was a "tour de force." As Superman, with makeup to deepen his skin tones and accentuate his eyes, and a padded costume, "he virtually exploded onto the screen," Salkind added. Nervous during the cab ride back to Heathrow Airport, Reeve confided in the studio driver, Bunny Barkus, who told him, "I've seen nearly the whole lot of 'em . . . and you've got the part."

Back in New York, Reeve tried to go about his normal routine. One morning in the third week of February 1977, his phone rang. Before Reeve could get the receiver to his ear he could hear his agent screaming that he'd just heard entertainment reporter Rona Barrett announce on ABC's *Good Morning America* that Reeve had been chosen to play Superman. Ilya Salkind called soon after to confirm. Reeve signed on for $250,000. The search for Superman, which had taken two years, had finally ended.

Superman, the character, was a Depression baby, created in Cleveland, Ohio, by cartoonists Jerry Siegel and Joseph

Shuster. Siegel, largely influenced by science fiction stories in pulp magazines and by Greek mythology, designed his brainchild to be more powerful than Hercules. In 1938, after numerous rejections, Siegel and Shuster sold their character to Detective Comics (now DC Comics). Superman made his radio debut with Mutual Network on February 12, 1940, played by Clayton "Bud" Collyer. Then Columbia Pictures brought him to life on the screen in 1948 (*Superman*) and 1950 (*Atom Man vs. Superman*), starring Kirk Allyn. By 1951 George Reeves had taken over the role, starring in 104 television episodes until 1957 and in one movie, *Superman and the Mole Men* (1951). With limited movie-making technology back then, the attacking Mole Men carried tricked-up vacuum cleaners as weapons. In 1953, Noel Neill joined the cast to play Lois Lane. Reruns of the television series continued to air for years.

As a comic book, *Superman* took on a life of its own.

Reeve as Superman stops a train from derailing. The actor was careful to make Superman a complex character with the "wisdom and the maturity" to use his powers for the benefit of humankind.

During World War II, American soldiers carried it in their duffel bags. According to authors Reinhold Reitberger and Wolfgang Fuchs in *Comics—Anatomy of a Mass Medium,* "[Superman] gave them hope and became their symbol of courage and determination, almost a substitute for conventional religion—to the horror of the Army chaplains." For so many GIs, raised in a religious tradition of "turning the other cheek" when attacked, the mythic, altruistic strong man who defeated seemingly insurmountable evil foes offered them a role model who fought back as they battled an enemy that fought with unbridled aggression and pursued a policy of genocide. But there was some irony in America's choosing Superman as a rallying icon: it was a German philosopher, Friedrich Nietzsche, who had coined the term "Superman" (*Ubermensch*).

When *Godfather* writer Mario Puzo submitted his six-hour script to the Salkinds in 1975, *Superman* was a dark and brooding Greek tragedy with heavy biblical overtones. Writers Robert Benton, David and Leslie Newman, and Tom Mankiewicz shortened and lightened the script. The final product remained true to the classic Superman story, in which he is sent to Earth by his parents Jor-El (Brando) and Lara (Susannah York) when their planet, Krypton, blows up. He is raised by Kansas farmer Jonathan Clark and his wife, Martha. As a youth, he is initiated into his true identity, living for 12 years in a crystalline fortress at the North Pole. At 30, he assumes the identity of newspaper reporter Clark Kent, going to work for the *Daily Planet* in the city of Metropolis, where he meets and falls in love with feisty fellow reporter Lois Lane. With superhuman speed and strength, he fights crime and even stops the earth's rotation, reversing time to save Lois Lane's life and prevent a massive earthquake from destroying the West Coast.

The tale, as envisioned by its writers, would take place in three parts, with the first two—set on Krypton and in Kansas—very serious in tone. Set designer John Barry was to render Krypton with chrome, white lights, and Plexiglas for a crystalline look, and cinematographer Geoffrey Unsworth would portray Kansas using broad, sweeping shots of wheat fields, farms, and wide-open skies. A sudden shift in tone to a quirky, comic-book style occurs in the third—Metropolis—part of the story. The shift is from the profound to the profane, with scheming archvillain Lex Luthor (Gene Hackman), bellowing *Daily Planet* editor-in-chief Perry White (Jackie Cooper), lusty Luthor consort Miss Tessmacher (Valerie Perrine), and gruff, chain-smoking Lois Lane (Margot Kidder). Metropolis, gray and noisy, is glaringly antithetical to the serene wheat fields of Kansas.

Reeve took the script along on the plane ride from New York to London to begin rehearsing his lines. As he pored over scenes in which Superman performed feats of strength, he realized that, at 180 pounds, his credibility would falter. One of Richard Donner's first directives to Reeve upon his arrival was to head to the Grosvenor Hotel in the posh Mayfair section of London. There, under the direction of *Star Wars'* David Prowse (Darth Vader), Reeve launched into a grueling body-building regimen, including an extra meal a day, protein milk shakes, and an array of vitamins. After a few weeks of hour-and-a-half workouts, Reeve had added more than 20 pounds to his self-proclaimed "stringbean" shape. In time he would go up to 220.

Now Donner and his crew would have to figure out how to make their Superman fly convincingly. They tested flying harnesses, hydraulic armatures, Chapman cranes, animated models, depressurized weightless chambers, underwater photography, and skydiving. For takeoff and landing shots, Reeve used trampolines. He insisted on doing most of his own stuntwork. "[He] is tremendously coordinated," John Barry said, "much more so than the acrobats and stuntmen we had. Plus he has nerves of steel. At some point he was 200 feet off the ground in the bitter cold. I asked him if that bothered him and he said that after the first 50 feet it didn't make any difference to him; he stopped caring about it."

Reeve also brought a convincing expression to his flying

shots because of his own experience as a pilot. "I'm a born flyer," he told *Newsweek*'s Jack Kroll. "I've got ratings in airplanes, seaplanes and gliders. I felt that although Superman's flying is made possible by the technicians, more than that, it's done in the eyes. You must see on a man's face a certain delight, a certain joy in flying that can only come out of inner conviction."

For Reeve, maintaining that expression while hooked up to his flying harness required enormous strength. The harness caused large bruises, which would eventually turn into calluses. While held aloft by the crane, he had to keep his arms and legs perfectly straight to prevent crabbing, or hanging in a crooked position while moving through the air. In December, when Reeve was to fly home for the holidays, the Superman flying technicians called Heathrow Airport and asked a British Airways employee to page him and announce, "Remember to keep your arms out straight and your feet together so you won't crab." They knew that Reeve, enormously shy about his Superman persona in public, would wilt with embarrassment at their joke.

Unlike other members of the *Superman* cast, Reeve maintained a serious demeanor throughout filming. Richard Donner and Gene Hackman would joke around between takes. Towering Jack O'Halloran, a former wrestler playing Non, a Krypton henchman, and vivacious Valerie Perrine would tap dance and sing while high atop crystal glaciers on the enormous Set E, which housed the Fortress of Solitude, Superman's Arctic retreat. But Reeve mostly kept to himself. After work he headed to bed early. "I'm not here to have fun," he told author David Petrou one day on the set. "I have a responsibility to see that [the film] is good. That's why I'm willing to make the sacrifices that I do . . . why I'm antisocial to the extent that I am. I come home every day from work sometimes in agony because I feel that a scene wasn't one hundred percent. . . . I guess I'm driven. I can't take screwing around. I can't take the lateness. I go nuts because I'm so rigidly focused into the work."

When asked what he did for fun, Reeve instantly brightened. "You see, when I work, I do nothing but work, and when I play, I do nothing but play," he said. He listed playing the piano, skiing, tennis, and flying planes and gliders as his "main vices."

Reeve did find some time during the filming of *Superman* to socialize, though. On the set he met British model Gae Exton, an attractive young woman with large blue eyes and long, light brown hair. They soon fell in love. At the time, Exton was estranged from her husband, David Iveson.

By the end of May 1977, Donner and the producers moved *Superman* production to the larger 100-acre Pinewood Studio Complex near the country village of Ives in Buckinghamshire. There, in an ivy-covered manor house, the director and producers worked out of a main office overlooking stately gardens and tree-lined pathways.

For exterior shots, the crew traveled to New York in July, shooting the *Daily News* Building, street scenes, and the Solow Building on Wall Street. Steamy, hot weather and unruly crowds made working there difficult.

But Reeve made his first public appearance in full Superman costume in New York on a relatively peaceful night. Writer David Petrou described the reaction of onlookers as Reeve was hoisted into the sky:

> Reeve was hooked into his flying rig and then he was fastened onto the end of a giant Chapman crane. Slowly, steadily, [he] was hoisted into the clear night sky . . . and suddenly heads turned, traffic stopped and a spontaneous thunderous burst of applause filled the air followed by cries of "Mommy, mommy look . . . it's Superman!" and "Hey, man . . . it's Superman!"
>
> And it was.
>
> Electrified by the crowd's enthusiasm, Reeve broke into a broad smile, seemed to glow . . . and waved back enthusiastically at the crowd.
>
> At that moment, surely, the producers must have realized they'd probably have a hit on their hands.

Clark Kent and Lois Lane (Margot Kidder) are accosted in a Metropolis alley in this scene from Super-man, the Movie. *Many critics who reviewed the film noted Reeve's graceful transitions from the mild-mannered reporter to the Man of Steel.*

From New York, most of the production moved on to Canada for the Kansas and North Pole shots. In September Reeve celebrated his 25th birthday back at Pinewood Studios by ironing out flaws in his flying shots. In his free moments he shared his thoughts on his role as Superman, the hero, with Petrou:

> A hero should not *know* he's a hero, otherwise he becomes pretentious and boring. With all the feats Superman does, if he says to himself, 'My God, am I good!' then you'd have a real prig, a boring piece of cardboard. So what I'm trying to do is go way under. If the script calls for incredible feats all I have to do is just simply do them. What makes Superman a hero is not that he has the power, but that he has the wisdom and the maturity to use the power wisely.

As filming continued, Donner gave Reeve the freedom to interpret the character as he wanted. Reeve liked playing up Superman's vulnerabilities. He also revealed his remarkable acting talent in the scene in which he drops off the thoroughly smitten Lois at her terrace after taking her flying around Metropolis. An instant later, a knock sounds at her door. The fumbling Clark peeks in the door, stuttering nasally, "Uh, Lois, we did have a, uh, date tonight, uh, remember?" While Lois goes off to comb her hair, Clark watches her, allowing himself to relax into his Superman identity. Magically, Reeve unhunches his shoulders, straightens, grows a full two inches, removes his overly large square glasses, smoothes the furrowed Clark Kent brow, thinks for a moment, then decides not to tell Lois who he really is. He smiles assuredly, with an expression of pride in his newfound love. Simply by shifting his body and his facial expression, Reeve achieves a complete persona switch, as if removing a mask.

Reeve extended his range in the scene when Lois is killed in a landslide during a Lex Luthor-induced earthquake. He tenderly lifts her body out of the rubble and caresses her cheek, but when she does not awaken, he kneels over her in silent agony. Finally, his face contorted with pain, he cries out to the heavens in his rage. In the scene Reeve convincingly shows both strength and gentleness—and then thunderous, godlike anger.

Meanwhile, Warner Communications, *Superman*'s financial backer, was issuing its own thunder, threatening to cut off funds at the scheduled production finishing date. With no end to production in sight, the producers decided to throw a wrap-up party to make it look like they were right on schedule. On October 28, their "End of Production Reception," as the invitation read, kicked off on a warm Indian summer day at Pinewood Studios. Reeve made his way through the lively crowd, which included business and financial backers, "smiling, chatting, shaking hands, looking relaxed in desert boots, jeans and an open-collar, white shirt with the sleeves rolled up," one on-the-scene writer wrote.

After flying home for the holidays, Reeve returned to Pinewood and went to work again. By March, the editing crew began their 12-hour-a-day, 7-day-a-week grind, selecting from thousands of feet of tape and constructing the necessary 380 opticals to create the effect they needed. In late April Reeve completed scenes on Stage C in which he appeared to be shooting through the earth's red-hot molten interior to fuse shifting tectonic plates. In August John Williams recorded his entire film score with the London Symphony Orchestra in England, and Reeve headed to Gallup, New Mexico, with Margot Kidder and Donner for final shots. Afterward he returned to Pinewood for a few more aerial stunts on the A Stage.

Finally, the time came. After three years of planning and two years of filming in three studios with 11 separate film units, in eight countries on three continents, with the work of over a thousand people in production, and at a record-breaking cost of nearly $40 million—*Superman* was ready to face the world. Reeve, Gene Hackman, and about 20 people from DC Comics sat in a cramped screening room for their first look at the movie. "Seeing it for the first time is like going on a blind date," he told one writer later. "I felt embarrassed, proud, remorseful and enthusiastic all at the same time." With two weeks to go before its grand opening world-wide, Reeve felt "overwhelmed with the feeling of the die having been cast. There was no turning back."

Moviegoers and critics around the world would decide the fate of *Superman, the Movie.*

Reeve poses with costar Margot Kidder at Superman, the Movie *'s Hollywood premiere in December 1978.* Superman *was greeted with rave reviews, and its young star was inundated with movie scripts—some of which he found objectionable.*

4

SOARING HIGHER, 1978–82

Go where your body and soul want to go.
When you have the feeling, then stay with it,
and don't let anyone throw you off. . . . You come to bliss.
—Joseph Campbell, *The Power of Myth*

IN MAY 1974, at 5:30 P.M., a small airplane droned along the beachfront of Cannes, France, site of the prestigious Cannes Film Festival. Trailing behind it, a banner read SUPERMAN in large letters. Festivalgoers taking a sunny break from darkened theaters were curious. The following year, three planes bearing the same message cruised lazily above the shoreline. In 1976 crowds in the same place gaped at a flying column of five planes, two helicopters, and one blimp, all announcing that *Superman* was coming—but when? By 1977, when a fleet of eight sailboats appeared out on the water, with each sail bearing a letter spelling SUPER-MAN, the crowd roared. By 1978, the Salkinds' beachfront show had become tradition.

Thanks to a massive worldwide promotion campaign, an eager audience awaited the film's release in December 1978. Crowds around the United States flocked to 700 movie theaters, and by the end of its first week the film had netted $12 million, the largest one-week gross in Warner Bros.' history.

Critics went wild about *Superman* and raved about Reeve. *Newsweek* ran a *Superman* comic-book-style cover, showing Reeve flying over Metropolis in Superman costume, his face stern and his hair so black it looked blue—just like the super-hero's. A headline in red type across the upper right corner read, "Superman to the Rescue." *Newsweek* critic Jack Kroll called Reeve "ridiculously good looking, with a face as sharp and strong as an ax blade," adding that "Reeve's entire per-formance is a delight." *Time* magazine wrote, "The easy au-thority with which Reeve handles the double role is the real surprise of the picture."

Reeve needed to come down to earth now that he had catapulted to almost godlike fame with *Superman*—and he needed a way to escape the devious side of show busi-ness. He went to sea. Like Ishmael in Herman Melville's classic *Moby-Dick,* who "drives off the spleen" by going "sail[ing] about a little and see[ing] the watery part of the world," Reeve put together a six-man crew and delivered a boat for its owner from Connecticut to Bermuda. "If you're out 500 miles off the coast of South Carolina and you see a force 10 gale coming, you know what you must do to sur-vive it," he told one writer. "[In] show business, people . . . play games. But on the sea or in the air, it's clear and it's di-rect, and it's simple."

Show business, however, had brought Reeve fame. "[*Super-man*] put me on the map," he told writer Sheila Alee. "It picked up the pace of my career about ten years. If I hadn't played Superman I'd still be climbing on [and off] Broad-way." The telephone at the Upper West Side apartment in New York that he shared with Exton rang incessantly for the next three months. Scores of scripts arrived from producers eager to snare a new box-office star. Reeve then made a de-cision that would set the tone for the rest of his career. In re-jecting $1 million to star in *American Gigolo* because he found the script "distasteful," he established a reputation for placing principle over dollars. He called the script "the de-piction of a lifestyle I don't believe in."

To his agent's dismay, he accepted instead a $600,000 role

in a low-budget Universal film, *Somewhere in Time,* based on Richard Matheson's 1975 novel, *Bid Time Return.* He said the film "offered a much more appealing, romantic sensibility," adding, "while it may err on the side of pretentiousness, [it] is an absolutely honest attempt to create an old-fashioned romance. It's based on love rather than sex or X-rated bedroom scenes."

Reeve began preparing to play the role of a young Chicago playwright, Richard Collier, who falls in love with the photograph of an actress from 1912. Collier travels back in time 67 years to meet her. Jane Seymour (*Dr. Quinn, Medicine Woman*) played the young actress.

"*Somewhere in Time* was the first script to come along that had a well-developed character who could hold his own as a human being in a story that would not alienate the new friendships I made with *Superman*," he told writer Aljean

Reeve turned down $1 million to star in American Gigolo *to play the lead in the romantic fantasy* Somewhere in Time *opposite Jane Seymour (left). Although this Edwardian love story languished at the box office, Reeve had no regrets about his decision.*

Harmetz in August 1979. He was filming on Mackinac Island, just off the tip of Michigan's Northern Peninsula. The island itself seemed like a place forgotten by time. Tourists and natives alike travel by horse, carriage, or bicycle, since the islanders eschew cars. Universal was allowed four trucks for filming and a small sports car for Reeve's character to drive.

Against a convincing period backdrop, Reeve wore an Edwardian suit as he ardently pursued a reticent Seymour. Most critics praised Reeve's performance but panned the film. "It was a failure in the sense that the critics killed it," Reeve told a *Philadelphia Inquirer* reporter in February 1981. He added that he did not regret making the film. "I liked doing it," he said. "I think it was a very worthwhile effort" even though it was "not the movie I would have liked it to be."

Somewhere in Time certainly did not hurt Reeve's reputation as an actor. Writer Aljean Harmetz described him in the *New York Times* as someone who "thrives on acting, exults in it, seems as bred to his profession as a foxhound to the chase."

Although his cinematic love story did not succeed, Reeve's real-life romance with Exton continued to blossom. Fans wrote to gossip columnists wanting to know if handsome Christopher Reeve was married yet. They were told that he was not, but was living with Exton as they awaited her divorce from her husband, which finally came through in November 1979. At that time, filming of Reeve's third major motion picture—*Superman II*—drew to a close.

The Superman contract that Reeve had signed called for two movies, but when the Salkinds fired Richard Donner and hired Richard Lester to direct, Reeve feared a drastic drop in quality. To help calm his fears, the Salkinds doubled his salary to $500,000 and hired the same writers who penned *Superman, the Movie.*

The story grew out of the opening scene of the first movie, when three Krypton criminals, the Hitleresque General Zod (British Shakespearean actor Terence Stamp); his elfin accomplice, Ursa (Sarah Douglas); and the oafish Non (Jack O'Halloran) were imprisoned by vote of Krypton's High Council. Their jail, a two-dimensional holographic square called the Phantom Zone, tumbles out into the universe. In *Superman II,* a terrorist's bomb, which Superman has cast out into space, explodes and shatters their prison, freeing them. After a stop on the moon to murder a joint American/ Soviet space exploration team, they take over Earth. Superman, off with Lois Lane in his Fortress of Solitude, is unaware of what has happened. He has chosen lovemaking over heroism and has relinquished his super capabilities. Upon learning of Zod and his evil accomplices' takeover of Earth, he (mysteriously) regains his power and outsmarts the Zod threesome and their accomplice, Lex Luthor (Hackman). In the end, Superman saves the Earth and rescues Lois from the torment of life apart from him by erasing her memory of their tryst.

Reeve and Gae Exton enjoy an outing in 1980. By this time, the couple, who met during the filming of Superman, the Movie, *were living happily together.*

Superman II was released in December 1980 in Europe and premiered the following June in America, but Reeve found himself partaking in his own drama on December 21.

At a private hospital in London, he assisted while Exton gave birth to their first child, a seven-pound, five-ounce boy whom they named Matthew. The new family greeted reporters in Exton's flower-filled room. But tabloids ran away with the news story, calling Matthew "Superbaby," which angered Reeve. "I'd be appalled if anyone called him [that]," Reeve fumed.

His irritation with the tabloids notwithstanding, Reeve continued to be greeted by good news. Critics loved *Superman II. Newsweek*'s David Ansen wrote, "Faster than a speeding bullet comes the verdict: *Superman II* is a success, a stirring sequel to the smash of '79," adding, "the comic heroic mixture [of characters] wouldn't jell without Reeve's sweet courtly presence at its center." Pauline Kael, film critic for the highbrow *New Yorker,* practically chortled through her review, calling the film "more sheer fun to see than anything else around." She echoed Reeve's own intent in doing *Somewhere in Time* when she added:

> Superman has old-fashioned virtue-charm. . . . His love for Lois Lane and his sense of responsibility toward her (and the whole country) . . . give the film its jokey yet touching romanticism.

Of Reeve's performance, Kael wrote, "Reeve has become a smoothie: his transitions from Clark Kent to Superman and back are now polished comedy routines." David Denby of *New York* magazine observed that Reeve was "openly enjoying his role, by showing an actor's pleasure in the notion that putting on glasses makes one a eunuch and taking them off a stud."

But the Academy of Motion Picture Arts and Sciences did not nominate Reeve for an Oscar for either of his Superman roles, nor did they invite him to become a member. *Chicago Tribune* film critic Gene Siskel called the slight "adding insult to injury" because Reeve played the lead in two of "the best selling movies of all time." Reeve had won the respect of the British Academy, though, which had given him its

Best Actor Award in 1979 for his role in the first *Superman.*

Following the success of *Superman II,* Reeve turned down a $1 million movie role and escaped the Hollywood star track by going back to the stage in Williamstown, Massachusetts, and to the revitalizing experience of acting serious dramatic roles before live audiences. At the Festival Theatre, for only $225 a week, he performed in three plays, Chekhov's *The Cherry Orchard,* Hecht and MacArthur's *The Front Page,* and a revival of the 1947 Broadway play *The Heiress,* based on an 1881 Henry James novel.

Taking a break from *Front Page* performances, Reeve flew from Williamstown to New York City one day for an appearance with film critic Gene Shalit on NBC's *Today Show.* Sarah Matthiessen, a reporter for *After Dark* magazine, found Reeve concentrating for the upcoming interview "in an absolute stupor . . . alone on a small couch staring at the wall." At interview time, Reeve took his place on the set and Matthiessen watched as Shalit, a peppery character with an exaggerated handlebar mustache, grilled the actor. Amazed, she watched Reeve demonstrate "a coruscating intellect and powers of speech uncommon in an actor." Off the set, Shalit ran over to Reeve, exclaiming, "What an interview! Boy, you can really talk!"

A studio chauffeur drove Reeve and Sarah Matthiessen to the Teterboro, New York, airport. There, he and Matthiessen climbed into one of Reeve's three planes and he executed a perfect takeoff. "If ease [were] a mask, it was impossibly secure," she wrote of Reeve as a pilot. He spoke of his other two planes, one parked outside London and the other in California. Yes, they were "signs of success," he acknowledged, adding that being rich "sure beats taking the bus." But he qualified success: it didn't mean leading "a magical life"; it meant more work and more friends—some of them sincere, some not.

As they flew, Reeve talked about Hollywood casting, producers, his favorite directors, and his future plans. He found theatrical casting preferable to Hollywood's, with theater

Costar Swoosie Kurtz (center) confronts Reeve's character, Kenneth Talley Jr., in the Broadway production of Lanford Wilson's The Fifth of July. *To play the crippled Vietnam vet, Reeve once again turned down a lucrative film offer in favor of following his own dreams.*

parts going "to the actor who's most qualified, regardless of [box office] impact." Reeve named his favorite directors, whom he called "the varsity": Alan Pakula, Sidney Pollack, Sidney Lumet, Michael Apted, Arthur Hiller, and Colin Higgins. He also praised directors David Lean and George Cukor as "the old masters." Reeve went on to say that he'd been asked to star in a Broadway production of Lanford Wilson's *The Fifth of July* in the fall. He intended to take the offer if the Screen Actors Guild strike was still on. "So I'm moving right along," he said, gazing into the horizon. The flight over, Reeve nosed his plane earthward and brought it to a "three-point perfect" landing.

To star in *The Fifth of July,* Reeve once again turned down a lucrative film role paying $1 million. His agent barely tolerated the decision. "He looked at it as a summer vacation and said, 'Well, you'll get all that theater stuff out of your system,'" Reeve told a *New York Times* reporter. By playing Kenneth Talley Jr., a Vietnam vet who was a double amputee and a teacher of handicapped children, Reeve did a complete about-face from playing an all-powerful hero. His new role also eerily foreshadowed his future. *The Fifth of July* was Wilson's sequel to his Pulitzer Prize-winning play, *Talley's Folly,* the story of the zany but tender courtship of a Missouri farm girl, Sally Talley, and her city beau, Matt Friedman. *The Fifth of July* takes place 33 years later, and Sally is "Old Aunt Sally." Friedman is long gone, and Ken and his left-wing '60s friends from Berkeley reunite at the Talley Farm on the night of Independence Day, 1977.

The role, for which Reeve wore plastic braces on his legs, called for him to display depression and inner turmoil. When the play opened on November 5, 1980, at the New Apollo Theater, some critics felt he had landed just shy of that mark. Frank Rich of the *New York Times* wrote that Reeve "works earnestly, and in the later scenes he lets us see some of Kenny's pain. But by then it's too late. His placid face never suggests someone who has lost his legs in the hell of Southeast Asia, and his voice lacks presence and maturity. At most, he gives us the wry surface of the character." But *Newsweek's* critic wrote that *The Fifth of July* deserved "at least the Nobel [Prize]," and that Reeve, "a young but committed stage actor" was "effective and winning as Ken." Despite mixed reviews, the play succeeded.

Reeve left the company, however, in April 1981 to costar as a nefarious student playwright in the film version of the Broadway hit *Deathtrap.* In this comedic thriller, a well-known playwright, Sidney Bruhl (played by Michael Caine, known for his performances in the movies *The Ipcress File, Alfie,* and *The Man Who Would Be King,* among others), having penned a slew of recent flops, decides to steal the perfect murder mystery play, written by his former student, Clifford Anderson (Reeve). Bruhl decides to murder Anderson as well. The two try to outwit each other amid a set of wild antique mechanical toys and instruments of torture in Bruhl's converted windmill home.

After the filming of *Deathtrap* was completed, Reeve spent his summer at the Williamstown Theatre Festival performing in Nikos Psacharopoulos' *The Greeks,* a two-evening, six-hour production of 10 plays based on Homer's *Iliad,* the epic tale of the Greek and Trojan War, and on the tragedies of Aeschylus, Sophocles, and Euripides. Reeve played Achilles, Greek hero of the *Iliad,* who killed his Trojan rival Hector and was himself killed by Paris, son of King Priam of Troy. Reeve, dressed all in brown as Achilles, overwhelmed the audience. Reminiscent of Superman, a cape hung over his left shoulder. It was as if Superman had gone back to his roots in his creator's memories of Greek legend and myth.

The plays chronicled a spiraling vortex of murder and revenge in the Trojan War, from the murder of Agamemnon by his wife upon his return, to the infanticide committed by Medea. Throughout these gruesome tales, mankind reels at the caprices of the gods, just as earthlings cowered helplessly before the evil machinations of General Zod, Ursa, and Non in *Superman II.*

After *The Greeks* opened in July, *Newsweek* critic Charles

Michener wrote that Reeve, "a low-flying Superman," was "among the standouts."

In 1981 Reeve earned the Ten Outstanding Americans Award from the United States Jaycees.

By the age of 30, his reputation and his career on the stage and in films was flying at an altitude approaching the cosmic heights of Superman himself. He seemed to have proven that he could weather just about any force 10 gale that show business and the critics blasted his way. Tempered and strong, he aimed for greater success.

Reeve is ready for danger as student playwright Clifford Anderson in the comedy-thriller Deathtrap. *In the words of critic Gene Siskel, Reeve and costar Michael Caine were "captivatingly theatrical" without being "a pair of hambones" in the film.*

5

SWITCHING CAPES, 1981–85

Two roads diverged in a wood, and I—
I took the one less traveled by,
And that has made all the difference.
—Robert Frost, "The Road Not Taken"

REEVE VENTURED INTO television acting for the first time since his portrayal of the arrant Ben Harper in *Love of Life* during the mid-1970s, only now he would portray a prince—a real one—in the cable network Showtime's production of "Sleeping Beauty," as part of its Faerie Tale Theater series. Reporter Sheila Alee found him on the set in South Carolina in 1981, with Superman on his mind. He told her that a third Superman script was being written and that if he considered it good he would star in it.

Deathtrap, released in March 1982, stirred up a flurry of praise for Reeve. *Newsweek*'s David Ansen observed:

> Making a movie out of Ira Levin's Broadway blockbuster *Deathtrap* was a perilous idea. Levin's witty contrivance, a comic thriller in the British tradition (in which *bon mots* are as lethally sharpened as the murder weapons), is just the kind of play that usually disintegrates under the scrutiny of the camera, its sophisticated turns brutally exposed as melodramatic claptrap. It didn't happen.

61

Instead, according to Ansen, *Deathtrap* turned out to be a "dandy little movie" and Reeve was "getting to show new facets of his talent." Gary Arnold of the *Washington Post* wrote, "He ingratiates himself in a fresh way by impersonating a charming menace, extending his range to the amoral, treacherous aspects of human nature." *Chicago Tribune* critic Gene Siskel marveled at the interaction of Reeve and Caine, giving Reeve the nod over the more experienced actor:

> These two actors tread a fine line between being captivatingly theatrical and simply being a pair of hambones. If I had to choose one performance over the other, I would choose Reeve's simply because he is so good at getting intensely angry without seeming silly.

Reeve went on to shock viewers in his next film, *Monsignor,* produced by Frank Yablans and directed by Frank Perry, in which he plays Father Flaherty, a corrupt American priest who schemes to make money for the Vatican and deceives and seduces a young nun, played by Genevieve Bujold. Filmed in Rome, *Monsignor* met with widespread condemnation by Catholics and critics alike when it was released in October 1982. Jack Kroll of *Newsweek* called it an "ecclesiastical geek of a movie" and warned that, like Father Flaherty, who conceals his identity from the young nun he seduces, Reeve might "permanently conceal his identity as an actor" with roles like this one.

Reeve returned once again to his Superman role. He approved of the new script for *Superman III,* and he agreed with the Salkinds to appear in the film for $2 million—and top billing. *Superman II* director Richard Lester returned for this sequel.

Reeve maintained a lighthearted approach to the role. In April 1982, just before filming started, he met with reporter Fred Yager, who noted that the doorbell of Reeve's Upper West Side apartment "never stops ringing." During the interview, third-graders from a nearby school called through his intercom, "Can Superman come out and play?" "Not today,"

Reeve bellowed, "He's got to save somebody." Reeve, laughing, told Yager that he often played Superman for friends as an intermediary between them and their children: "A lot of kids who are having trouble talking to parents will talk to me. I have a certain trust, through Superman, and I can open things up. It's a safe territory." Reeve added that he wanted to enhance his alter ego's image, emphasizing Superman as a gentleman, instead of a "machismo bullet-stopping wall."

But Lester shattered the pure image of Superman as a gentleman in *Superman III*. Reeve was called upon to play not only the two roles of Clark Kent and Superman, but also a third role—Superman gone bad. Archvillain Ross Webster, played by former television series star Robert Vaughn (*The Man from U.N.C.L.E.*), uses the computer wizardry of goofy computer nerd Gus Gorman, played by comedian Richard Pryor, to control the world's oil supply. Gorman syn-

Monsignor, released in 1982, had the dubious distinction of being condemned by both critics and the Catholic Church. Reeve played Father Flaherty, an unscrupulous American priest who becomes the central figure in a Vatican scandal.

thesizes a not-quite-pure chunk of glowing green kryptonite, which he cons Superman into accepting as a public service award.

The impure kryptonite does not kill Superman, but it does cause a Jekyll-Hyde split in his personality, creating an evil Superman who performs such pesky deeds as blowing out the eternal Olympic flame, punching a hole in an oil tanker to cause a spill, abandoning accident victims, and sexually harassing high school sweetheart Lana Lang (Annette O'Toole). He even hangs out in a sleazy bar and smashes glasses by hurling peanut missiles. In a rather flawed movie, Reeve offers a stunning performance as the warring sides of Superman—physically manifested as Clark Kent and Super-man—battling for control in an auto junkyard. As the evil Superman, he contorts his face with rage to create a char-acter who looks more like a soul possessed than a superhero.

Critics generally disliked *Superman III,* which was re-leased in mid-June 1983, largely because of the film's purely comic-strip tone, which was a far cry from the mythic grandeur of the first two films. They also hated what Lester had done with Superman himself. Pauline Kael wrote in *The New Yorker:*

> Superman/Clark Kent (Reeve), who grew into a touching character in *Superman II,* is presented here as a blank—he's whatever is needed to fit the gags. Clark Kent is a bore with a simpering grin and Superman has been doing good deeds for so long that the people of Metropolis take him for granted.

Kael admitted that the film is entertaining when Superman does perform heroically, but complained that "the splashy scenes we look forward to don't seem to show up." David Denby of *New York* wrote that the "startlingly sexy" aspect of evil Superman was "a good idea that should have been developed." Jack Kroll of *Newsweek* was one of the few critics who had something good to say about *Superman III,* finding "the idea of a schizoid, alienated Superman . . . funny and weirdly touching," and calling the movie "cute" and "clever" but "without the audacity of Richard Donner's *Superman.*"

The media had long since latched onto the sex appeal of Reeve himself, and *Newsweek* had featured him in a cover story called "The Incredible Hunks" just before *Superman III* was released. Reeve appeared in the story with popular actors Richard Gere (who starred instead of Reeve in *American Gigolo*), Tom Selleck (of the TV series *Magnum, P.I.*), Mel Gibson (then best known for his performance in the film *The Year of Living Dangerously*), and Harrison Ford (*Star Wars*).

Reeve's good looks attracted women like a magnet. Stories spread of his involvements outside of his relationship with Exton. Further fueling speculations and gossip, Reeve disagreed with Exton over a prenuptial agreement that she would not sign. It stipulated that Reeve would pay child support if they were to divorce, but not alimony, because Exton had her own means of support in the form of her modeling agency.

Reports in the media implied that Reeve was on the verge of breaking up with Exton. (Yet early the next year, the couple announced that they were expecting another baby.) They still had no wedding plans, however. Natalie Singer, Reeve's secretary, told one reporter, "Everyone assumes that because Exton is having another child that they will wed, but they have no plans to marry."

Reeve's career had taken wing in the summer of 1983. Producers Ismail Merchant of India and James Ivory of California, noted for their high-quality films, asked Reeve to co-star in their film adaptation of American novelist Henry James's 1886 novel, *The Bostonians,* which explored what was then called "the woman question": suffragettes' struggle to achieve equality and the right to vote. Nineteenth-century Boston was considered a mecca for intellectual, liberal activists like the abolitionists who fought slavery before the Civil War.

Reeve's character, Basil Ransome, embodies both the sexist male establishment and the defeated South. Ransome, who sports shoulder-length hair and a mustache, is a Mississippi gentleman from a plantation-owning family. Impoverished after the Civil War, he travels to the North in 1875 to become a lawyer. Reeve leapt at the chance to play a serious dramatic film role, hoping to at last "escape the cape," a phrase he had turned while filming *Somewhere in Time.*

He actually traded the red Superman cape for another one: the long dark cloak typical of a gentleman at Ransome's time. Reeve costarred with British actress Vanessa Redgrave, who played the role of Basil's cousin, Olive Chancellor, a venerable Boston "bluestocking" (scholarly lady). Olive takes Basil to the home of a Mrs. Birdseye for women's suffrage meetings. There, both he and Olive fall in love with a young, innocent, impassioned orator, Verena (Madeleine Potter), who is hypnotized by her father before each public appearance. Olive wants to foster Verena's "gift" for "the cause," while Basil wants only to take her away from the women's movement, which he calls a "modern pestilence." He sees women as inferior to men and argues that they should be private and passive.

As before, Reeve passed up a high-priced movie role in favor of this serious dramatic part. When he turned down an offer of $1 million to star in the action-packed thriller *The Bounty,* accepting only $120,000 for *The Bostonians,* he and his agent quarreled and parted ways. "I wanted to be an actor, not run around with a machine gun," Reeve told an *Entertainment Weekly* writer.

In his usual perfectionist manner, Reeve prepared for his part by reading the novel four times and by studying Leon Edel's biography of Henry James. He also mastered a Southern accent by listening to the recorded speeches of Mississippi lawyer Haley Barbour, who later became head of the Republican National Committee.

Reeve followed up filming of *The Bostonians* by flying off to Yugoslavia to begin shooting his next film, *The Aviator.* Throughout the shooting, he and Exton remained apart, she living in London and he working on various film locations. When she went into labor, Reeve flew back in time for the birth of their daughter, Alexandra, who was almost exactly four years younger than her brother, Matthew. While their relationship seemed untroubled again, Reeve and Exton still had no plans to wed.

The Aviator, based on the popular Ernest Gann novel and directed by Australian George Miller, featured Reeve in a part that seemed perfect for him: a seasoned airmail pilot, Edgar Anscombe, who flies over treacherous mountain territory in the late 1920s. Reeve flew the plane himself, did his own stunts, and—in his first time behind the camera—directed scenes of his character's struggle to survive after Anscombe's plane crashes into a mountain and he is attacked by wolves.

The Aviator failed to get off the ground. Initial screenings drew such poor responses that Metro-Goldwyn-Mayer/United Artists limited its release to only a few theaters in 1985.

But Reeve rebounded in another Henry James role.

Vanessa Redgrave, who would earn her second Academy Award nomination for her role as Olive Chancellor in *The Bostonians,* called Reeve before Christmas in 1983 and asked if he would like to costar in the London stage production of James's novel *The Aspern Papers.* Reeve jumped at the offer, once again passing up lucrative film jobs to do so. Redgrave's father, Sir Michael Redgrave, had made the play famous in 1959 when he produced, directed, and starred in it. Vanessa was staging it again in his honor.

Reeve flew to London and rehearsed with the cast, which included the 71-year-old legend Dame Wendy Hiller. After two months of rehearsal, he opened—once again with shoulder-length hair, a mustache, and period costume—at the Princess Grace Theater in Monaco. On March 8, 1984, the play opened in London to astounding reviews. The theater critic for the *New Statesman* wrote that he had expected

the presence, but not the depth and detail of Reeve's protagonist, Henry Jarvis. Standing and sitting with the deliberate formality of a Victorian portrait, his size will always make him something of a Superman, but in this case, his charisma is charged with a ruthlessness that is both repellent and fascinating.

The *London Observer* hailed his "star entrance," saying that, as Jarvis, the "ruthless American scholar," he arrives with a

British actress Vanessa Redgrave and Reeve in a relaxed moment. After she costarred with Reeve in the critically acclaimed The Bostonians, *Redgrave was so impressed with Reeve's talent that she asked him to join her in the London stage production of* The Aspern Papers *less than one year later.*

predatory pounce upwards into the Venetian *sala* of Miss Bordereau and her niece. Don't ask me how anyone can pounce upwards . . . but [that] is exactly what Mr. Reeve does. . . .

It is, physically and psychologically, a marvelous moment and compels in an audience anxious to clap whenever they can, a chilled and electrifying silence. . . . Mr. Reeve remains watchable throughout.

Reeve went on to revel in accolades for his earlier James

performance as Basil Ransome when *The Bostonians* premiered two months later at the Cannes Film Festival in May
1984. When it opened in New York later that month, many
critics greeted it with high praise and credited Reeve as a
talented actor. *The New Yorker*'s Pauline Kael, however, found
fault with the production. Kael had read the novel before
seeing the movie—as Reeve had before playing his part—
and she had envisioned the novel's Ransome as a "bitter"
man who was "replaying the Civil War, determined that this
time the South would win." She noted with disappointment
that Reeve's Ransome was instead "pleasant" and "fun to
watch," and that the "bird cage" life he offers Vereena "seems
rather jolly" instead of confining.

Critic David Sterritt sided with Reeve's representation:
"Reeve, trading his Superman cape for a nineteenth-century
model, is the soft-spoken Basil down to his toes," and he
called *The Bostonians* "the best movie I've seen all year."

Reeve had done it. He had found success bringing a serious dramatic role to the big screen. What's more, on the
stage, he had dared to play a part made famous by the revered
Sir Michael Redgrave, and in doing so, had pleased not only
British audiences but the British press as well.

Reeve, who so often chose lower-paying roles that met
with his high standards of quality, found that taking "the
road less traveled by," as his father's friend Robert Frost
wrote in his poem "The Road Not Taken," "had made all the
difference" in terms of personal satisfaction. In the years to
come, Reeve would continue to stick to his principles and to
try in his own life to make a difference—to make the world
a better place.

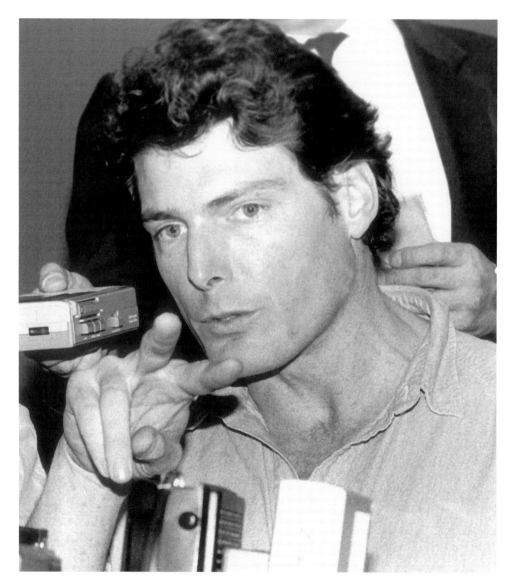

Reeve answers reporters' questions about his daring journey to Santiago, Chile, which he took on behalf of a group of Chilean actors who were scheduled for execution. The actors were marked for death because they had satirized the Pinochet regime.

6

HERO, 1984–88

*There are two types of deed. One is the physical deed, in which
the hero performs a courageous act in battle or saves a life.*
—Joseph Campbell, *The Power of Myth*

AFTER HIS BRILLIANT success in two Jamesian roles, Reeve went
back to Williamstown in the summer of 1984 to play Ned Seton, an alcoholic, in Philip Barry's *Holiday* and then to perform in a new play, *Richard
Corey,* based on a poem by Edwin Arlington Robinson. Reviewers hailed
the play. Reeve's performance brought an invitation to continue the role
on Broadway, but he declined.

Reeve then found that the red cape he thought he'd left behind still
colored his identity as an actor when he sought and lost the role of a
teacher of the deaf in the film *Children of a Lesser God.* The producers
felt that the public still identified him too much with Superman and gave
the part to William Hurt.

So Reeve traveled back in time again, playing the role of Count Aleksey Vronsky in his first telemovie, a CBS adaptation of Tolstoy's 1877
novel, *Anna Karenina,* a tale of a woman's search for love beyond an un-
fulfilling marriage. Filming took place in Budapest, Hungary.

The beautiful Jacqueline Bisset, a longtime favorite of Reeve's, played
Anna. Paul Scofield, a well-known British actor, played her husband,

Karenin. In the story, Anna falls in love with Reeve's character, Vronsky, who rejects her when she becomes pregnant with his child. In the end, disgraced and bereft, Anna throws herself to her death before an oncoming train.

Anna Karenina has graced the screen many times, first in 1935 with the old-time greats Greta Garbo and Frederic March in the lead roles. So Reeve and Bisset faced an audience with high expectations of their performances. Reeve, as usual, prepared obsessively for the part, reading all of Tolstoy's writings. Perhaps his father's expertise in Russian literature prompted him to bring as much authenticity to the part as possible.

Critics were hard on him, though, when the film aired on March 26, 1985. *Variety*'s Jeff Jarvis wrote that in a role calling for passion, Reeve showed emotion only for his dead horse and none for Anna when she told him of her pregnancy. But Monica Collins of *USA Today* said, "Reeve's Vronsky has the perfect pitch of the love-lorn naif—youthfulness, extravagance, and crass opportunism." Up against some popular sitcoms the night it aired, *Anna Karenina* did not attract a large audience.

By now, Reeve had acquired three homes: one in Martha's Vineyard, one in Hollywood Hills, California, and his apartment in New York. He also had three airplanes and a 40-foot yacht. His cost of living ran very high, but starring in television movies paid much less than did movie roles. When Reeve sought the lead in the film *The Running Man,* he lost it to Arnold Schwarzenegger. He threw himself into more television projects to earn much-needed income, hosting a 1984 PBS documentary titled *Vincent—a Dutchman* about the artist Vincent van Gogh, and hosting and narrating another special, *Dinosaur!* in 1985. In the coming years, Reeve would take on other minor projects: hosting a documentary called *Space Flight* (1987) and making audio recordings of *The Secret Path* (1989) and *The Great Gatsby* (1992). He also hosted a one-hour drivers' safety special sponsored by Valvoline Oil Company (1989).

Yet he still appeared each summer, for a paltry fee, in the Williamstown Theatre Festival because of his love for performing there. In 1985 he starred in the George Kaufman–Edna Ferber comedy *The Royal Family* and headed to his Martha's Vineyard home for a family vacation afterward.

He and Exton were growing apart. They spent only half the year together: her modeling agency, her new work as a casting director, and Matthew's private schooling kept her in London much of the time. Perhaps sensing their impending split, Reeve offered praise for Exton and criticized himself as "a romantic dreamer" who lived in extremes. "I'm sometimes instinctive, impulsive," he told one writer. "But Gae has the ability to ground me, to make me see things more realistically," he told one writer. "She's consistent, whereas I tend to be moody. I blow hot and cold."

As Count Aleksey Vronsky, Reeve woos the title character (played by Jacqueline Bisset) of Anna Karenina. *The CBS television movie, an adaptation of Tolstoy's classic 1877 novel, tells the story of Anna's attempt to escape the pain of a loveless marriage in the arms of Vronsky.*

When Exton and the children headed back to London in the fall of 1985, Reeve took off for New York to play Count Almaviva in *The Marriage of Figaro,* a French comedy written by Beaumarchais and first performed in Paris in 1784. Director Andrei Serban used Richard Nelson's adaptation to create a vaudevillian spectacle out of the old play, with actors wheeling about onstage on roller skates, skateboards, wheelchairs, cars, bikes, and casters. Serban's production infuriated some theater critics. "[He] . . . mutilates beyond recognition a play that has given satisfaction for decades, perhaps centuries," Brendan Gill wrote in *The New Yorker.* "The cast . . . has my sympathy." John Simon of *New York* called the production "vulgar, tasteless and cheap." Gill apparently disliked the performances as much as he had the production values, saying that the Count's infatuation with Figaro's betrothed, Suzanne, was "lacking in plausibility."

In good and bad reviews alike, critics usually linked Reeve with Superman. He never really seemed to "escape the cape." Although he had vowed never to do another Superman movie, Reeve was again offered the chance to play Superman—when he most needed the paycheck that came with a major film role. The offer came from Menahem Golan and Yoram Globus, two Israeli cousins who had bought the rights to the Superman films from the Salkinds. Reeve's agent, Jim Wiatt, suggested that he make a deal with the producer/directors for $4 million: $3 million for the Superman part, including complete control over the script as well as a portion of the directing; and $1 million to make another movie of Reeve's choice beforehand. Golan and Globus agreed, and Reeve chose his first film, *Street Smart,* a story about an ambitious journalist who makes up an award-winning story about a pimp in New York City and almost loses his life. With Jerry Schatzberg directing, filming took place in Harlem and Montreal. Scriptwriter David Freeman, a former writer for *New York* magazine, based the story on his own experience of fabricating a similar news story—and of paying the price.

Reeve's character, Jonathan Fisher, first calls on prostitutes like Punchy, played by Kathy Baker (*Picket Fences*), who are willing to ply their trade, but unwilling to talk about their pimps (bosses). So Fisher makes up his own story, which nets him media fame and the offer of a high-paying television news job. A district attorney thinks Jonathan's fictional pimp, "Tyrone," is a real-life felon called Fast Black (Morgan Freeman), who is being prosecuted for murder. Fast Black forces Jonathan to provide him with an alibi. Jonathan nearly becomes the victim of his own lie, until he can outwit his deadly coconspirator. Reeve shared his thoughts about taking the role of such an unprincipled character with a *Los Angeles Daily News* reporter:

> I'm interested to see if the audience will accept me as a weasel in the film. . . . Life is not about good guys and bad guys. It's about people trying to survive, it's about personal ethics versus the pressure to succeed. I felt it would be interesting to play a man who is really quite lost, very weak, dishonest, and stupid in many ways.

In his own life, Reeve had faced a more mundane version of Fisher's dilemma. He too had made concessions to "survival," having just signed a contract for money he badly needed to play a role—Superman—he no longer wanted to play.

To prepare for the role of Jonathan Fisher, Reeve accompanied New York vice cops on their beats, befriended prostitutes and pimps, and, unlike Jonathan Fisher, gained a lot of valuable tips from them on their way of life. Halfway through filming, Reeve collapsed with an attack of appendicitis and had to undergo emergency surgery. Two days later he rejoined the crew, asking for no special treatment—just that his assailant in a fight scene avoid punching his abdomen.

Street Smart opened to mixed reviews in April 1987. But Morgan Freeman's performance netted him an Oscar nomination and the compliment "the greatest American actor" from Pauline Kael for his "classic performance."

After filming for *Street Smart* ended, Reeve flew from

Canada to Vermont late in the summer of 1986 to take up politics for the first time in his life. He campaigned for the reelection of U.S. senator Patrick Leahy, a liberal environmentalist, who had hoped to garner more votes by adding Reeve's name to his campaign. When Reeve flew his own plane into Burlington for a rally, an enthusiastic crowd awaited him. He praised Leahy for his efforts toward arms control and for his stand against aid to the Nicaraguan contras, a right-wing guerilla group fighting to overthrow the Central American nation's Communist government. Leahy soundly defeated his opponent Richard Snelling that year.

Then it was time for Reeve to play the very role he no longer wanted to play—Superman. He moved on to England and the Cannon studio at Elstree in Hertfordshire. He cowrote the script with Lawrence Kohner and Mark Rosenthal for the fourth Superman movie, which they called *Superman IV: The Quest for Peace.* Reeve called in Gene Hackman, Margot Kidder, Jackie Cooper, and Susannah York from the first film to play their original parts. The respected Sidney J. Furie (*The Ipcress File*) replaced Lester as director. Young Mariel Hemingway played the daughter of the *Daily Planet*'s new owner; she falls in love with Clark Kent. Lois Lane rekindles her affection for Superman, who by the story's end gathers all the world's nuclear weapons, hurls them into the sun, and lectures the United Nations on world peace.

When the movie opened in August 1987, it confounded the critics. "From its opening shot—a Soviet cosmonaut singing [Frank Sinatra's theme song] 'My Way' in Russian as he works on an orbiting satellite—the first half of this film is sheer delight," a *People* critic wrote. But there was a problem with the second half: "There isn't any," the critic continued. "Even at 91 minutes the film seems truncated. One minute Superman is cowering in his apartment, the next he is zooming off triumphantly into the credits." The writer speculated that Kohner and Rosenthal had run out of ideas, saying that it was "unlikely" that Golan and Globus "ran out of money." But that was exactly what had happened. When

"I'm interested to see if the audience will accept me as a weasel in the film," Reeve said of his deci-sion to play misguided reporter Jonathan Fisher in 1987's Street Smart. *He got mixed reviews as a less-than-heroic character.*

their funds ran out, they simply released the unfinished movie. Reeve had realized his brainchild was doomed. Yet he persevered with the filming because of his contract, and because the other actors' and the production crew's jobs depended on his presence. It was a frustrating winter that was going from bad to worse.

During this time Reeve and Exton ended their nine-year relationship. Reeve purchased a house for her in England as a farewell present. But he was reluctant to discuss the breakup. He eagerly talked about himself and his children during an interview with Michael Bandler for *McCalls,* though. He confessed to being "an action junkie" who would take off at any time to fly in his twin-engine Cessna, sail along the English coast, ski, or mountain climb. Reeve went on to say that he hoped Matthew, seven, and Alexandra, three, would come to the United States for high school. "I trust the communication between Gae and me will be good enough so that we can work out whatever's best for the kids at the time. For now they understand that they have two homes and that they'll be fully loved and accepted in each."

In the summer of 1987, Reeve, 35, headed back to the world he loved so well, the theater at Williamstown, Massachusetts, and the mountainside home he had built for himself the summer before. He starred in a sex farce called *The Rover,* playing a rogue called Willard. After his performances he would head to a nearby restaurant, the 1886 Williams House, which had an after-hours cabaret. Sometimes he sang there.

On the night of June 30, he made a discovery that would forever change his life. That night, as he sat in the audience, a young woman with straight honey-colored hair, large brown eyes, a wide grin, and a matter-of-fact manner got up on the stage and sang Cole Porter's "It's Delovely." Reeve stared, riveted by her mirthful, sparkling eyes. Who was she? He had to know.

She was 26-year-old Dana Charles Morosini, a young actress from Scarsdale, New York, a graduate of the Institute of the Arts in Valencia, California, and a first-year performer

Gae Exton, Christopher Reeve, and son Matthew in happier times. This picture was taken in 1982: by 1985, there was clearly a rift in the couple's relationship, despite the arrival of daughter Alexandra in 1984. They spent much of their time apart, with Exton in London and Reeve away filming or on theatrical tours.

at the Williamstown Festival. Reeve decided he had to meet her. After her performance, he approached her and asked her to go to the Zoo, a nearby nightclub. She refused a ride with him, but said she'd meet him there. Before she left, her friends warned her that Reeve was "on the make," but when she met up with him at the Zoo, she suddenly found him "irresistible," she later told a reporter for *People* magazine. "We ended up talking for an hour," Reeve said. "We didn't get a drink, we didn't sit down, we didn't move. Everything just vanished around us."

A "ten-day courtship of flowers and long steamy looks" followed, Reeve told the *People* writer. One night Reeve invited Morosini for a moonlight swim at the nearby Margaret Lindley Pond. She suspected seduction, but was relieved—and hooked—when he offered to pick up her swimsuit. "I thought he was so sweet. That night was our first kiss," she said. Reeve picked June 30 as their "anniversary" date, and the two of them made "It's Delovely" their own song and sang it as a duet when friends requested it.

Reeve often invited Morosini to his Williamstown home, which lay on 36 acres of farmland. There he stored his glider, cross-country skied, raised livestock, and fished in his own pond. Reeve also became interested in learning to ride thoroughbred horses and purchased some. On the days when he and Morosini wanted to go to sea, he would sail his 46-foot yacht, the *Sea Angel,* which he had built to accommodate his height.

In November they moved in together. Their worst conflict arose over tidiness habits: "My side of the bed is neat. Hers looks like a yard sale," Reeve told *People.* "Sometimes it gets to me and I say, 'Clutter alert.'"

On November 22, Reeve received a phone call that would test his courage. Ariel Dorfman, a writer whose editorial protesting the abominable cruelties of the Augusto Pinochet regime in his native Chile had just appeared in the *New York Times,* told Reeve that the Pinochet death squads had ordered 79 of Chile's top actors, directors, and playwrights to leave the country under pain of death for satirizing the Pinochet regime. The death squad, Trizano (named after a Chilean who had hunted down and killed thousands of native Chileans a century before), claimed that the entertainers were Marxists. Dorfman asked Reeve to go to Chile and head a rally on behalf of the actors to halt the action of Trizano. The presence of a major star, especially one known around the world as Superman, they reasoned, would bring international attention to their plight. Reeve, knowing his life would be in danger, considered the request for a half hour and called Dorfman with his decision: yes, he would go.

Accompanied by Dorfman's wife, Angelica—who served as his interpreter—Reeve traveled to Santiago, Chile's largest city. When they arrived on November 30, 1987, a cartoon in a local paper portrayed Superman carrying Pinochet off in his arms.

The actors were to be executed within 24 hours. Operating without the protection of the United States government, Reeve acted under the aegis of Amnesty International and the Actors' Equity Association.

The gravity of the situation hit home when Reeve saw young actors walking the streets of Santiago wearing T-shirts with red bull's-eyes that read "Shoot me first." Visiting the home of one actor, Julio Jung, Reeve was shocked to discover that Jung was receiving threatening phone calls with bursts of machine-gun fire sounding in the receiver. The rally, set for eight o'clock that night, was scheduled to be held at a stadium in a poor section of town. But when thousands arrived chanting, "Superman, Superman—take Pinochet away," police dispersed the crowd. The organizers found a second location, an old airplane hangar with only one door, which was 10 feet wide. Several thousand protesters packed into the building. Fully realizing that he might be killed if he entered the building, Reeve forged ahead, fighting his way to the stage, while the crowd screamed, "Superman, Superman." "It was unbelievable," Reeve said later, "the kind of reception I'd associate with the Pope, or the Beatles at Shea

Stadium." Police outside were trying to break up the crowd formed by those who hadn't been able to get in.

The crowd sang, "He [Pinochet] will fall" as Reeve got up to speak. Lights went out, but all remained calm. When the lights were restored, Reeve held up a letter signed by several top American actors: Gene Hackman, Cher, Martin Sheen, Susan Sarandon, and Mia Farrow. With no microphone, he read the letter in a loud stage voice. When he finished, he told the crowd that he would tell America "what brave and beautiful people you are." The following day, the Pinochet leaders retracted the execution order.

Ariel Dorfman said, "Reeve is an example of how one can relate his art to his life. Chileans can never be thankful enough for his presence there that day." Reeve maintained a humble attitude afterward: "This was not Superman to the rescue," he told a *Los Angeles Times* reporter. "It was me as a private citizen, and as an actor in a country where we take the freedom to perform for granted, helping fellow professionals in a country where they do not. If you know me as Superman, fine, but we have to remember that Superman is light entertainment. This was real life. This was not just an adventure story; this was not in the comic books."

Pinochet's government was ousted a year later. Dorfman said, "It was very difficult to get rid of Pinochet. And it's fair to say that Reeve was at least partly responsible for his removal." The Walter Briehl Human Rights Foundation, a group of psychotherapists who work with torture victims, bestowed upon Reeve two awards for his bravery in 1988.

Up until this point Reeve had contributed his energies outside of acting and his hobbies to protecting the environment and helping impoverished children, among many other causes. Now he had proven himself a hero, far transcending the fictional heroism of Superman. He once told a writer his own definition of a hero: an ordinary person who risks his or her life to honor deeply held principles. Reeve had become that kind of hero.

In his journey to battle the murderous dictator Pinochet,

Reeve put concern for his own life aside, and in doing so, he found himself. In that harrowing process, Reeve emerged as a person united with those who seek justice and freedom throughout the world. He also emerged as a hero of the mythic type that inspired the creation of Superman.

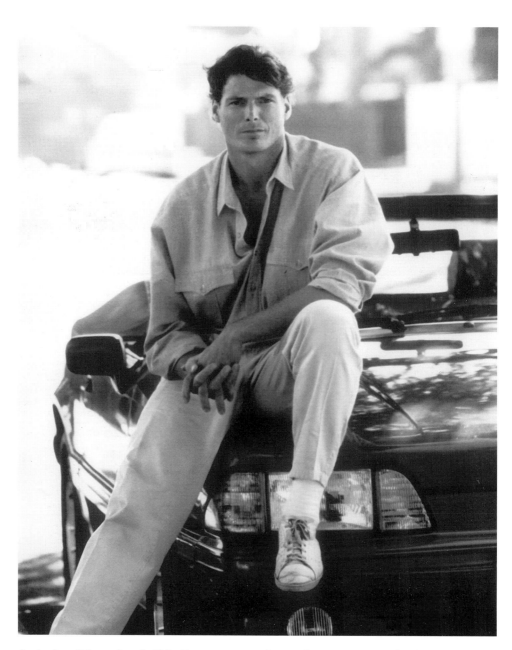

In the late '80s and early '90s, Reeve continued to perform on stage and in films but turned increasingly to network and cable television for work. He is shown here in a promotional shot for "The Valvoline National Driving Test," a program on driver safety, which he hosted for CBS in 1989.

7

FINDING LOVE AGAIN, 1988–95

Shall I compare thee to a summer's day?
Thou art more lovely and more temperate.
—William Shakespeare, Sonnet 18

AS REEVE APPROACHED his forties he continued to expand his range of roles, but he lost his position as a top choice for leading roles in major motion pictures. Allowing himself room to experiment as an actor, Reeve costarred as a nerdy, acrophobic (afraid of heights) blonde millionaire in the movie *Switching Channels.* As Blaine Bingham, owner of a chain of sporting-goods stores, he tries to lure Christy (Kathleen Turner) from her job as a broadcast journalist and from her dictatorial news manager (Burt Reynolds)—who also happens to be her ex-husband. Screenwriter Jonathan Reynolds fashioned the story after the 1928 Ben Hecht–Charles MacArthur play *The Front Page.*

Reeve found himself in familiar territory. He had coached British actors at the Old Vic in American English during a run of the play in London when he was in college and had later performed in the play at Williamstown. Jonathan Reynolds's screenplay marked *The Front Page*'s fourth film facelift, but when the film opened in March 1988, critics seemed to prefer the original. Peter Travers of *People* charged that the screenwriter had left out the play's "wit and character," adding that di-

Reeve turned to all-out comedy in 1988's Switching Channels. *As high-strung millionaire Blaine Bingham, he woos TV anchorwoman Christy Colleran (Kathleen Turner), much to the consternation of her ex-husband and boss, Sully Sullivan (Burt Reynolds). Although critics generally dismissed the film, they noted Reeve's ability as a character actor.*

rector Ted Kotcheff's idea of having the cast talk rapidly, after the manner of the "screwball comedies" of the 1930s, was a "crucial error." The movie did not gross well at the box office, but film critic Jeffrey Lyons called Reeve's Blaine Bingham "his best role."

That spring Reeve performed in a Tennessee Williams play, *Summer and Smoke,* at the Ahmanson Theater in Los Angeles, playing the alcoholic ladies' man John Buchanan Jr. opposite Christine Lahti (*Chicago Hope*). One reviewer wrote that his performance "even shines in the scenes where he's particularly cad-like."

Although Reeve told one writer he was looking for a "big, big, big hit" toward the end of 1988, none came. In the meantime he turned to television with the same gusto that he brought to his film roles. NBC offered him the opportunity to play Major John Dodge, one of the masterminds of a famous 1944 escape from a German prison camp, in the TV movie *The Great Escape II: The Untold Story.* Steve Mc-Queen had first brought the role of Dodge to the screen in the 1963 classic *The Great Escape,* one of Reeve's childhood favorites.

In his meticulous fashion, Reeve prepared for the role by reading a book on Dodge that his mother recommended. From that, he learned that Dodge's daughter lived in England and he contacted her. He learned from her that Dodge, American born, grew up in England and became an explorer and an adventurer—and a man of honor. Several times he escaped the prison for the sole purpose of investigating the surrounding countryside and then allowed himself to be recaptured so he could share what he had learned with the other prisoners planning the escape.

When the miniseries aired on Sunday, November 6, it drew a fairly large audience. But the second episode, which aired the following night, lost some viewers to *Monday Night Football.* Critic Jeff Jarvis, missing the action-packed, "zowie" effect of the less accurate 1963 movie, wrote that he found the miniseries "monotonous." But Michael Hill responded favorably to the production, writing, "Filmed in Yugoslavia, it has a nice look, a feeling of reality aided by evident attention to detail."

After *The Great Escape II,* Reeve took time to help a very special cause. Williamstown's movie theater, Images Cinema, was going to be razed by developers. To save the theater, Reeve gathered fellow stars to host screenings of their films, and they raised $50,000. His plan worked. The old movie house was converted to a smaller screening room with space for new stores.

He then fought the construction of a $350 million coal-burning electrical power plant in nearby New York because he feared it would pollute the Berkshire Hills. His actions "played a significant role in the apparent defeat of that project," according to one Sierra Club member quoted in the Williamstown *Advocate.*

Reeve still waited for Hollywood to notice him, accept-

In 1988 Reeve got to reprise the role Steve McQueen made famous in his boyhood favorite, The Great Escape. *He prepared for the role of John Dodge in* The Great Escape II: The Untold Story *by contacting a daughter of Dodge's who was living in England. Costar Michael Nader is on the right.*

ing minor television projects to fill his diminishing bank accounts. He reported on the destruction of the Amazon rain forest in a one-hour PBS program and hosted "The World's Greatest Stunts."

Fortunately, Reeve had kept alive his stage career, which sustained his soul. But there too he found his share of derisive critics. He played the supporting role of Polixenes, childhood friend to Mandy Patinkin's (*Chicago Hope*) Leontes in Joe Papp's production of Shakespeare's *The Winter's Tale* at the Public Theater in New York. When the show opened in April 1989, Reeve drew comments like "all profile" from Moira Hodgson of the *Nation*. The *New Republic*'s Robert Brustein noted that Reeve possessed "a stately aristocratic bearing, but also a muted naturalistic delivery that robs him of forthrightness and resolve."

Offstage, Reeve continued to effect positive social change and to impress people in high places with his integrity. While working with his New York civic group, Westpride, to prevent millionaire Donald Trump from building a large development called Trump City on the West Side, Reeve turned down an offer to narrate a documentary on Trump. The program was funded by Trump's enemy, developer Leonard Stern; Reeve feared it would be grossly inaccurate. Trump wrote to thank Reeve for his selflessness in forfeiting a paying job in the name of fairness. He then met with Reeve and agreed to a compromise: a project that would fit in better with the West Side ambience.

In the summer of 1989, Reeve returned to Williamstown to successfully perform a dual role: a Northerner and a Southerner in the Civil War play *John Brown's Body*. *New York Times* critic Mel Gussow hailed Reeve's performance, writing that he brought "great conviction" to his part. Gussow also wrote that the play opened the Williamstown season "on a note of eloquence."

Perhaps some of Reeve's onstage pathos reflected his grief over the death earlier that year of Williamstown's founder and his friend and mentor, Nikos Psacharopoulos. If Williamstown was Reeve's "first home" as he later told one writer, then Psacharopoulos was the centerpiece of that home. The loss shook Reeve's world.

But his sense of responsibility in the world outside the theater led to an ever-expanding activist role. "The global issue will be the future of the planet as a place to live," he said in an interview. In 1990 he recorded public service announcements promoting a proposed New York state law that would enable the public to sue polluters. He narrated *Black Tide,* a Discovery Channel documentary on the *Exxon Valdez* oil tanker spill off the coast of Alaska; he said that there had been 43 spills in that vicinity, which were continually killing wildlife and destroying the ecosystem. Soon after, he traveled to Washington to urge lawmakers to pass the Clean Air Act. On April 3, 1990, it became law.

The following month, at his 20th Princeton Day School reunion, Reeve accepted his class's Alumni Award for his volunteer work with some 30 charitable causes. Headmaster Duncan Alling cited Reeve as an example for the school's students, who were required to do community service work.

He had recently garnered high praise in his national tour of A. R. Gurney's *Love Letters* opposite Julie Hagerty. The role called for him to be charming, but also to suffer an emotional breakdown by the play's end. Kevin Kelly of the *Boston Globe* called his performance "wonderful" and wrote that his portrayal of the character Andy was

> closer . . . to the essential pathos at the heart of Gurney's script [than any other actor's]. The emotion in Christopher Reeve reading the final apostrophic letter, the tears streaming down his face . . . there's nothing more I can tell you. [The play] gets more remarkable each week. . . . I can't imagine it without Reeve and Hagerty.

After a fund-raising tour for AIDS victims, Reeve once again went to Williamstown in the summer, this time to play the Grim Reaper opposite Blythe Danner in *Death Takes a Holiday,* a 1929 Broadway hit. Again critics liked his performance. Mel Gussow of the *New York Times* wrote that he was "a not-so grim reaper." "More than anything, it is the actor's drollness that helps invigorate this creaky vehicle," he added.

Reeve took up the cause of beleaguered artists, as he had before in Chile, traveling to Washington in the spring of 1990 with other actors from the 225-person Creative Coalition that he had cofounded with actress Blair Brown. The coalition counted among its members Susan Sarandon (who would later win the Academy Award for best actress for *Dead Man Walking*) and Alec Baldwin (*Ghosts of Mississippi*). Reeve and his fellow coalition members spoke with Congress about the National Endowment for the Arts (NEA), which conservatives like Senator Jesse Helms and television evangelist Pat Robertson were attacking because they felt that some

Mr. Reeve

NEA artists were publicly displaying obscene creations. They wanted NEA grant recipients to sign a pledge agreeing not to create works that would be offensive in nature. *McCalls* magazine printed Reeve's position on the issue in January 1991. He explained that the NEA, in its 25 years, had supported 85,000 artistic productions throughout the United States, including the Vietnam Memorial, Pulitzer Prize-winning plays, arts education in schools, and educational performances by major symphony orchestras in rural towns. "Politicians should *never* have the authority" to censor artists, Reeve argued. In October 1990, the Creative Coalition's lobbying efforts paid off: "Congress decided that the NEA's critics should not be given official status as the moral guardians of America, and that politicians not be empowered to decide what is art," Reeve said.

Despite his political and theatrical successes, Reeve still had to turn to television for an income that hardly matched

As copresident of the Creative Coalition, Reeve fought to make the National Endowment for the Arts a priority on Capitol Hill. He is shown here in 1995 with (left to right) Massachusetts senator Edward Kennedy, Vermont senator James Jeffords, and Charleston, South Carolina, mayor Joseph Riley Jr.

his old movie salaries. In the 1991 TV movie *Bump in the Night,* Reeve played a role that would horrify Superman fans, but which he hoped would educate parents of young children.

He portrayed a former college literature professor, who, after being released from jail for child molestation, kidnaps the son of a divorced alcoholic journalist (Meredith Baxter, formerly of *Family Ties*) with the same intent. Reeve told *Washington Post* writer Patricia Brennan that he would not let his children (Matthew, 11, and Alexandra, 7) see the movie until they were much older. "In fact I didn't let either of my children come to the set," he said.

Playing the role brought back the memory of a similar incident in his own life. When he was 13 a photographer taking publicity shots of him suggested he take his shirt off. "I went straight home and told my parents," Reeve said. He related his insights about his own experience to the development of his movie character:

> Because nothing specifically had happened to me, there was no arrest that could be made. Apparently pedophiles move in on children from broken homes.

Reeve cautioned again that the movie is "for adults to watch and not for children. One of the messages is to account for children's time. Don't let your child slip away from you." Brennan wrote of Reeve's performance: "The charming manner in which he beguiles his intended victim is chilling."

In his next telemovie, *Death Dreams,* Reeve got top billing as a husband jealous of his stepdaughter, whom he fails to revive after he rescues her from drowning. She dies and appears to her mother many times after the mother has a near-death experience following a car crash. *Variety* called the two-hour teledrama "skillfully produced" and "credible," adding that the special effects were "tops." Reeve, as the "ill-tempered, ruthless financier" was "believable."

Reeve also won praise for his next TV performance, this time as an architect "pressured to compromise his ideals for business" in *The Last Ferry Home.* "Acting is on the mark,"

Variety magazine said. "Low-key Reeve is supported by one of the best casts assembled for a locally produced drama."

Reeve finally did net a cinematic film role, playing with his former costars Michael Caine and Julie Hagerty and with the legendary comedienne Carol Burnett in a film version of *Noises Off,* a British farce by Michael Frayn about the backstage tomfoolery of an acting troupe. Peter Bogdanovich directed. The story is a play within a play, in which Reeve portrays the owner of a house, and Burnett, his slovenly housekeeper. *Variety* critic Todd McCarthy wrote that Reeve had "no problem as the dunderheaded leading man whose trousers are often caught around his ankles." Stanley Kaufman wrote in the *New Republic* that he "is limber as the husband and is appealingly ridiculous backstage as the actor who plays the husband." Another reviewer called Reeve's performance "top rate." Despite good reviews, *Noises Off* failed to take off at the box office when it opened in March 1992.

For his next telemovie, *Mortal Sins,* Reeve donned the cassock again to play Father Cusack, a priest stalking a serial killer who admits to each murder in the confessional, binding Cusack to silence. Eventually Cusack brings the cynical daughter of one victim back to her faith, and he nabs the killer. Tony Scott called Reeve's performance "smooth as pudding."

In his private life, Reeve was finding Morosini the perfect mate. He had told one writer two years earlier,

> One of the things that's so great about Dana is we sail together, we dive together, we ride together. She skis . . . as well as I do. . . . She plays a good game of tennis. She's a great dancer. She laughs all the time. She thinks life is to be enjoyed. So I've got a partner.

But when asked about marriage plans, he revealed his reasons for avoiding it. "I think that I've had a hard time, since growing up I saw a lot of marriages that didn't work," he explained. "The impression I got of marriage as a child was that marriage is not a stable institution. People make promises they don't mean and they don't keep."

But with Morosini, Reeve came to change his ideas about marriage, and about trust. One April night in their Manhattan penthouse, during a candlelit dinner of turkey and meatballs, they locked eyes "virtually at the same time," he recalled later, and both said, "Let's get married." They set a June wedding date, but Morosini held off on wedding dress fittings because she was seven months pregnant with their child—a boy, according to a sonogram reading. When they announced their plans, Morosini was performing in the Broadway play *Sight Unseen*. Reeve apparently stunned himself with his decision; he told writer Jeannie Park that he often waltzed around the house singing, "We're getting married!"

The wedding took place much earlier, because they learned that Morosini would deliver sometime in June. So on Saturday afternoon, April 11, 1992, they wed amid the pastoral beauty of Field Farm in South Williamstown. Matthew, 12, and Alexandra, 8, served as best man and the maid of honor,

By 1992, Reeve knew that in Dana Morosini (shown here playing pool with Reeve), he had not only a romantic partner but a companion who enjoyed many of the same things he did. He overcame his wariness of marriage that year and wed Morosini in a spring ceremony.

and all parents—Franklin and Barbara; Charles Morosini, an internist; and Helen Morosini, a publishing executive—joined the celebration. Before them and 45 other guests, Reeve, 39, and Morosini, 31, exchanged vows they had written for each other.

The Reeve-Morosini civilization had begun.

In the first week of June, at the North Adams Regional Hospital near Williamstown, Dana gave birth to their son, whom they named Will. Not wanting to raise Will in New York City, the new parents bought another home, a 19th-century farmhouse on seven acres near Bedford Village in New York's Westchester County, not far from Dana's parents' home. But they headed up to the Williamstown home in the summer. Reeve was looking forward to a visit from Matthew, who went to tennis camp there, and Alexandra, who liked to ride with him.

Reeve found time in 1992 to work for Bill Clinton's presidential campaign. He approved of the Arkansas Democrat governor's ideas and he strongly sided with vice presidential candidate Al Gore's pro-environment policy. "I've watched in despair as every environmental law is trashed by [the Bush-Quayle administration]," he told reporters. After Clinton won the election, he invited Reeve to address his inaugural gala. Reeve spoke of the fight to maintain the National Endowment for the Arts. "With the Clinton-Gore ticket," he declared, "the life of the artist is not something to be ashamed of anymore."

Reeve completed filming another telemovie, *Nightmare in the Daylight,* which aired on CBS on Sunday, November 22. A review credited him—as a husband seeking his wife, who was lost in the 1985 Mexico City earthquake—with "playing well through some naturalistic domestic scenes," despite a poor script and inadequate direction.

Reeve went on to play a San Francisco writer, Hump, in a telemovie of Jack London's 1904 novel, *The Sea Wolf.* Hump is rescued from the San Francisco Bay by the crew of a sealing schooner called *Ghost,* which was captained by a miscast Charles Bronson. *Variety* magazine found Reeve's portrayal of the writer-turned-cabin boy "credible" but panned the overall production.

Reeve merited strong critical praise for his role in a small movie about the Great Depression, *Morning Glory,* playing opposite Deborah Raffin. The film did not succeed, but Gene Seymour of *Newsday* had glowing praise for Reeve:

> The strong but silent patina, harder to pull off than it looks, seems a perfect fit for Reeve. . . . This movie isn't big enough to make Reeve a star again. But the impression he makes here is good enough to suggest that a reversal of perception —and fortune—won't be long in coming.

Reeve found that reversal when Merchant and Ivory—the producer/director team who had made *The Bostonians* and who had since expanded their market appeal with two lush E. M. Forster adaptations, *A Room with a View* and *Howard's End*—offered him a role in their new film, *The Remains of the Day.* It was to be an adaptation of Kazuo Ishigoro's 1989 novel. The story centered on a butler, Mr. Stevens, played by Academy Award-winning actor Anthony Hopkins (*The Silence of the Lambs, Howard's End, Nixon*), who submerges his own identity beneath that of his role as servant to his master, a British lord named Darlington. Stevens hangs on at the manor house after Darlington is disgraced for supporting the Nazi regime during World War II. Events leading to the war come up only infrequently as the housekeeper, played by Academy Award winner Emma Thompson (*Howard's End, Sense and Sensibility*), tries in vain to foster a relationship with Stevens.

Reeve portrays an American congressman named Lewis, who in 1936 tries to warn Darlington and his houseful of aristocratic friends that they are out of date in the new era of "Realpolitik," which calls for professional politicians. The story, told in flashbacks, opens with Lewis moving into the Darlington manor, which he has bought after the war.

Reeve was thrilled at the chance to act with the talented

Hopkins and Thompson. He gives a tour de force performance in the lavish banquet scene, wearing a tuxedo and tails, as he watches, tense and annoyed, while the French diplomat announces he is "impressed" by the Germans' attempts at peace. Lewis jumps to his feet, proposes a toast, and then levels the group with a deadly serious look and announces, "Now, excuse me, I have to say this. You are amateurs. And international affairs should never be run by gentleman amateurs. . . . The days when you could just act out of your noble instincts are over." Eyes widen; Darlington looks as if he has been slapped. Lewis hits his stride, and with a deepening voice and deadening aim, he continues his verbal assault.

"Christopher Reeve brings authority and Yankee energy to the one dissenting voice in the collaborationist circle," a *Variety* critic wrote when the film opened on the first Friday of November 1993. Critics celebrated the film, which earned eight Oscar nominations.

Movie scripts came Reeve's way again.

First he chose MGM's romantic comedy *Speechless,* playing the supporting role of a veteran TV war reporter nicknamed "Baghdad Bob," who tries to lure his old girlfriend (Geena Davis) back into his arms. The film, which tells of the awkward romance between two political speechwriters, played by Davis and Michael Keaton (*Batman*), failed to achieve the "madcap hilarity of the '40s romantic comedies it seeks to emulate," one critic noted after its December 1994 opening. "Few of the supporting players get the opportunity to shine," he added. Yet Janet Maslin of the *New York Times* wrote, "The story's sidelines are especially enlivened by Christopher Reeve." Still another writer concluded that Reeve had evolved into a "versatile character actor" and predicted, "It's only a matter of time before he's 'officially' rediscovered and celebrated, like John Travolta in *Pulp Fiction* this year."

In 1994 Reeve also managed to shoot a PBS special on gray whales in the waters off Anchorage, Alaska; to narrate a concert production of Rodgers and Hammerstein's musi-

Reeve's supporting role as Congressman Lewis in The Remains of the Day *revitalized his feature film career. His character is the only American among a gathering of European aristocrats in pre–World War II England.*

cal *Allegro;* and to host a Williamstown Theatre Festival 40th Anniversary celebration, reading passages from *John Brown's Body* and *Love Letters* with Julie Hagerty.

He took top billing in his next movie, playing Alan Chaffee, a town doctor who delivers a host of mind-controlling children, in Universal's *Village of the Damned.* Chaffee discovers a way to block and to terminate the powers of the blond-haired, green-and-red-eyed children. After its April 1995 opening, critics all but terminated this "risible" remake of a 1960 British sci-fi classic. Todd McCarthy of *Variety* called the film "a theatrical in-and-outer" and implied that "dull direct[ing]" had made poor use of Reeve's talent.

Throughout the ups and downs of his revitalized movie career, Reeve continued to champion the things he believed in. After filming *The Remains of the Day,* he flew to Tucson, Arizona, to defend a high school faculty advisor who was fired for staging the Pulitzer Prize- and Tony Award-winning 1977 play *The Shadow Box,* about three cancer patients confronting death. Parents objected to graphic language and suggestions of homosexuality. In the name of free speech, Reeve led actors Mercedes Ruehl, Blair Brown, Harry Hamlin, Estelle Parsons, Robert Sean Leonard, Michael Tucker, and Jill Eikenberry to perform the play in a local auditorium. An audience of over 600 rose to loudly applaud their performance. Reeve participated in a panel discussion the next day in which he argued against censorship.

In the spring of 1995, he led the Creative Coalition in an advocacy day that prepared the members for a trip to Capitol Hill to convince their representatives once again to save the NEA. With conservatives in control of Congress, they faced an uphill fight. Congress voted to cut arts funding by 40 percent—but not to kill the NEA. Reeve called it a "moral victory."

Reeve's career prospects looked bright. He was to star in a Francis Ford Coppola adaptation of Robert Louis Stevenson's pirate tale *Kidnapped.* In the spring, he had just finished filming an HBO action film, *Above Suspicion,* in which he played a detective who becomes paralyzed in a shootout and asks his wife and brother to kill him, saying, "Something inside me has died. I can't live my life as half a man."

Little did Reeve know how chillingly prescient this role was.

"Jumping is the most dangerous thing I do," Reeve once said. Although the sport is not for the faint-hearted, Reeve was a careful horseman, walking his mount over a new course many times before riding.

8

A Fallen Hero, 1995

The dream of flight is suddenly gone. . . . Freedom escapes you again,
and wings that were a moment ago no less than an eagle's,
and swifter, are metal and wood once more, inert and heavy.
—Beryl Markham, *West with the Night*

FILM PRODUCERS OFTEN required Reeve to sign contracts that contained "no flying" clauses to avoid the risk of his being injured—or worse—in a crash. In recent years, Reeve's producers had also called for "no horse jumping" clauses for the same reason. "Jumping is the most dangerous thing I do," Reeve himself once said in an interview.

Free from any film contracts with this jumping restriction at the end of May 1995, Reeve entered a three-day Commonwealth Dressage and Combined Training Association competition in precision horsemanship in Culpeper County, Virginia. He arrived at the Commonwealth Park equestrian facility, a 200-acre spread of light forest and green fields, on Friday, May 26. He then walked his 12-year-old thoroughbred chestnut gelding, Eastern Express, whom he called Buck, around the cross-country course, checking for any shadows or hidden depressions in the ground. Preparing for the competition as thoroughly as he would ready himself for a dramatic role, Reeve walked Buck around the course four times—twice what most other equestrians would do. On the sunny Saturday of May 27, he led Buck around the course once more, dressed himself in his blue and silver riding colors, cream-colored breeches, knee-high boots, safety vest, and hard riding helmet. Swinging up onto the saddle, he led Buck out to the warm-up area and rode around until his turn to compete arrived.

When his turn came, Reeve nudged Buck's flank with his spur to quicken his pace and leaned forward, preparing for the first of 15 jumps. With grace and style, rider and horse soared over the first two obstacles and cantered toward the third. Reeve had been practicing with Buck for several hours a day over several months. Veteran horse trainer Lisa Reid stood among the nearby bystanders and watched Reeve and Buck head toward the third jump, an easy one only three feet high that was a zig-zag formation of log rails.

"The horse was coming into the fence beautifully," Reid later told a reporter. "The rhythm was fine and Reeve was fine, and they were going at a good pace." Reeve leaned in close to Buck's neck, ready to jump. Then, according to Reid, Buck "put his front feet over the fence, but his hind feet never left the ground." He stopped suddenly. An onlooker later speculated that a rabbit might have spooked the horse.

Reeve's six-foot-four, 215-pound body, carried forward by momentum, fell over Buck's head. His hands were caught in the bridle, taking it and the reins and bit with him. His head first hit the rail, then, unable to break his fall with his hands, he struck the ground forehead-first, according to Reid. She ran to him and found him unconscious: motionless— and worse—not even breathing.

Another bystander, an anesthesiologist, saved Reeve's life by giving him mouth-to-mouth resuscitation until paramedics, who were on the scene in case of emergencies, could reach him. They immobilized his head and neck and painstakingly moved him onto a stretcher and to an ambulance, and then rushed him to the Culpeper Medical Center. There doctors confirmed everyone's worst fear: Reeve had shattered the first and second cervical vertebrae—those closest to the skull. He had damaged his spinal cord, the bundle of 20 million nerve fibers that runs through the center of the spine and carries impulses between the brain and the body. Unlike nerves in other parts of the body, those along the spinal cord cannot regenerate in the event of damage. To prevent further swelling of his spine—and still more damage to his spinal cord—he was given methylprednisolone, a synthetic steroid.

Christopher Reeve, a powerful, agile athlete still best known around the world as Superman, lay paralyzed from the neck down. He could not even breathe without a respirator. No scriptwriter could edit out this horrible twist in the story of his life.

Dana, staying with three-year-old Will at a hotel near Commonwealth Park, rushed to the Culpeper Medical Center after receiving a phone call alerting her to the disaster. Paramedics prepared to transfer Reeve to the University of Virginia Medical Center in a Medevac helicopter. Before takeoff, Dana was told to say good-bye to Reeve—just in

After Reeve was taken by helicopter to the University of Virginia Medical Center in Charlottesville for neurosurgery, reporters gathered outside for updates on his condition.

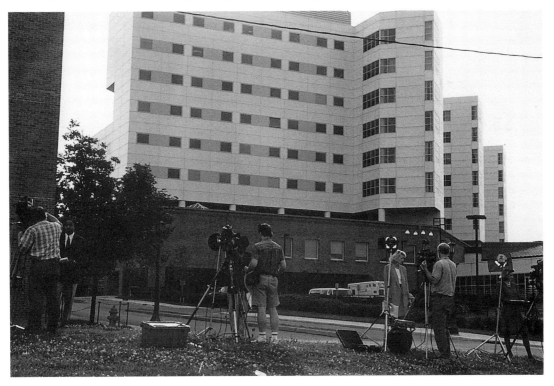

case. Little Will, seeing Reeve unconscious, feared his father would die. The helicopter took off for the 45-mile flight to the center in Charlottesville. Hours later, Reeve's neurosurgeon, Dr. John Jane, announced that Reeve had not suffered brain damage.

On May 31, Reeve regained consciousness and remembered nothing of the accident. He needed surgery, but doctors had to wait for antibiotics to clear the pneumonia that had developed in his lungs. His head had been placed into a metal ring with screws and weights to hold it immobile. Despite morphine injections, Reeve would periodically panic and try to snap his head from side to side; only additional morphine would settle him down. Reeve knew the exact extent of his injuries and realized that he might not survive the operation. He later told a journalist,

> When they told me what my condition was, I felt I was no longer a human being. Then Dana came into my room and knelt down to the level of my bed. We made eye contact. I said, 'Maybe this isn't worth it. Maybe I should just check out.' And she was crying and she said, 'But you're still *you, and I love *you*.' And that saved my life.

Will, along with Alexandra, 12, and Matthew, 16, who had just flown in from London with their mother, came into the room. "How can I possibly leave them?" Reeve thought.

On June 1, Reeve was in his hospital room "hanging upside down in bed." He later recalled looking up and seeing a blue scrub hat and a yellow gown, and hearing a Russian accent. "There was Robin Williams being some insane Russian doctor," Reeve remembered. "I laughed, and I knew I was going to be all right." Williams, his Juilliard School roommate, launched into a zany routine of comic one-liners, complimenting Reeve on his "new tie" (his respirator tube).

While Dana, Robin Williams, and Reeve's family held his will together, Dr. Jane prepared to mend his broken body. In a six-and-a-half-hour operation on June 5, Jane tied together the first and second vertebrae, wedging a bone graft

Dr. John A. Jane, the University of Virginia neurosurgeon who repaired Reeve's shattered first and second vertebrae, then fused the first vertebra to his skull. This procedure enabled Reeve to begin his rehabilitation.

from Reeve's hip between them, and fused the skull to the first vertebra with titanium wire. Afterward, Jane told reporters the operation would allow Reeve to "begin his mobilization" to sit up and, hopefully, "to begin his early rehabilitation."

From the day of the accident, Reeve's and Dana's emotions had vacillated wildly as Dr. Jane first told them Reeve was a "C1 incomplete"—that his spinal cord was all right and he could improve; then a "C4"—he might be able to move his arms; then a "C2 complete"—no possible improvement. "Complete" meant that the spinal cord was so damaged it could never be repaired. Finally, to their great relief, Reeve had some feeling in his neck and chest after the operation. This indicated that his spinal cord was not completely severed. Jane upgraded him to "C1 incomplete" once again. There was hope.

The love and concern that Reeve had given to the world in his political and environmental campaigns surged back to him in his moment of need. By the end of June, 20,000 letters and cards, more than 200 bouquets, children's drawings, books, videos, posters, and promises of prayers and special masses had arrived from friends, fans, politicians, Hollywood and theater people, and spinal-cord injury victims from all over the world. One electronic mail message read,

> You are a Superman and you will pull through this like the hero that you are. . . . I've come miles since [my spinal-cord injury], and life is every bit as enjoyable and worthwhile as it ever was. . . . Please don't give up. You have much to offer the world. . . . There are a lot of people out there pulling for you.

"Much of [Chris's] day is spent listening to messages sent from well-wishers," Dana read in a statement to the press and the public on June 9 at the University of Virginia Medical Center. "I can't begin to express how important these are to him. . . . He and I and the whole family are overwhelmed and truly honored by the affection and respect that have been expressed." She went on to note that President and Mrs. Clinton had sent good wishes, and she gave an update on her husband's condition: "[His] spirits are for the most part quite good." He was enjoying watching hockey on television with his family, which prompted Dana to quip, "I think his spirits might be better if the Rangers were in the playoffs." She then opened her heart to the world and shared her love and admiration for her husband:

Chris is a man blessed with extraordinary inner strength. He is a passionate man, committed to doing things well. I can't think of a challenge that he has not met . . . with fervent gusto. He is a fighter and a survivor of the first order.

Every day, although Reeve had no feeling in his hands, Dana clasped them and touched him affectionately, often singing the song "This Is a Pretty Planet" by John Forster and Tom Chapin, which they both had sung to Will. Later, during a television interview with Barbara Walters, Dana sang the song for Reeve. She took him by the hand, looked lovingly into his eyes, and sang softly to him; a vulnerable Reeve, grinning, looked up into her eyes, his own brimming with tears.

By the end of June, Reeve was well enough to be moved to the Kessler Institute in West Orange, New Jersey, for re-habilitation. In his first few weeks there, he found that the delicate hold he had on life could sever in an instant. Lying in his private room one night, Reeve suddenly had no air to breathe: the tube bringing air from the respirator through a hole in his trachea had popped out, cutting off his air sup-ply. When a security guard responded to the alarm on the ventilator, Reeve could only make clicking noises in his throat to indicate what was wrong. Unfamiliar with the device, the guard left to find a nurse. "I thrashed around," he said later, "I wanted air. I was like a tuna fish landed in a boat, rolling around with the hook still in my mouth." A nurse arrived to reinsert the tube—just in time. Another time, Reeve was injected with Sygen, an experimental drug for spinal cord injuries. He instantly displayed symptoms of an aller-gic reaction: he wheezed, he could not take air into his lungs, his heart rate soared and his blood pressure plummeted to 40 over 20. "I felt the way you do when you've been diving too deep and you think you're not going to make it to the surface," Reeve later told a writer. He thought, "I'm sorry, but I have to go now," and felt "embarrassed for having failed, for not having been able to win the struggle," he said.

But just then, Dr. Steven Kirshblum, director of Kessler's Spinal Cord Injury and Ventilator program, arrived and gave Reeve a large dose of epinephrine and "jump started" his heart, Reeve said.

These harrowing episodes over, Reeve then faced the day-to-day challenge of accepting his condition and learning to take charge of whatever improvements he could make beyond simple shoulder shrugs and neck movements. On July 13, Kessler's chief medical director, Dr. Marcia Sipski (a psychiatrist), told reporters that Reeve had "done something fantastic": he had learned to speak using the air he exhaled from his ventilator.

As the weeks wore on, Reeve struggled through his regimen of respiratory, physical, occupational, and speech therapies. His medical team—a psychologist, a nurse, a pulmonologist (lung specialist), a hematologist (blood specialist), a social worker, and a psychiatrist (Dr. Sipski)—monitored his progress and encouraged him along the way. Each day he spent break time in his wheelchair with Dana outside on the institute's wooded grounds.

One day he found himself called upon to lead a battle beyond the terrain of his own physical limitations. Another spinal-cord injury victim, Arthur Ullian, who was paralyzed from the waist down, came to visit him. Ullian told Reeve about his efforts over many years to convince national lawmakers to allocate more funds to spinal cord injury research—and now wanted to recruit Reeve to head the campaign. Then Henry Stiffel, chairman of the American Paralysis Association, called on Reeve and found him interested in his organization because "they are dedicated solely to finding a cure for paralysis, nothing less," Reeve said later. "I liked that ideal. They're not [just] into lower sidewalks and better wheelchairs." He knew that with his contacts in high places, he could bring tremendous clout to the cause. One of his caretakers told him, "You've been in the grave two times this year, brother. You're not going there again. You are here for a reason."

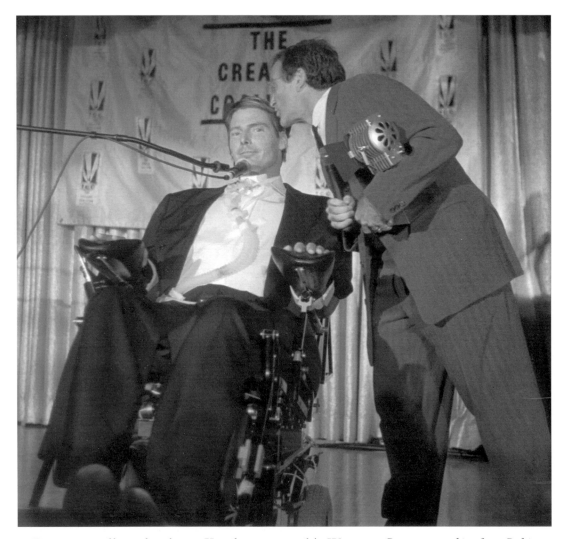

Reeve was allowed to leave Kessler to go to his West-chester home for his 43rd birthday. It was his first time home since the accident. As the van pulled up to the driveway, "I had a moment when the tears let loose," he told writer Liz Smith. But he adjusted. "Wait a minute," he said to himself. "So I've got a ramp. It's not the end of the world."

He left Kessler a second time to make his first public appearance at a Creative Coalition dinner in honor of Robin Williams at New York City's Pierre Hotel on October 16.

Reeve gets a kiss from Robin Williams as he makes his first public appearance since his accident to present Williams with a Creative Coalition award on October 16, 1995. Months earlier, Williams had lifted the bed-bound Reeve's spirits with his impersonation of a mad Russian doctor.

Dressed in a tuxedo and his ventilator "tie," he entered the ballroom in his electric wheelchair and was greeted with a five-minute standing ovation. Speaking in measured intervals, Reeve told the crowd why he had come: he had once had an English teacher who would accept only one excuse for missing class—"a quadruple amputation. So I thought I'd better show up." Laughter rippled through the assembly. He then introduced Dana, telling the audience, "I owe her my life," and then Williams, who addressed Reeve seriously: "You're on a roll, bro," then added with a grin, "Literally."

Reeve, with Dana beside him, sat by a fireplace at one end of the room, surrounded by his friends. Susan Sarandon joked with Robin Williams. Bobby Kennedy Jr. and his wife, Mary, and New York mayor Rudolph Guiliani came to wish him well. "Being here signals the beginning of the rest of his life," Creative Coalition copresident Blair Brown told a reporter.

After this successful outing, Reeve returned to Kessler for more rehabilitation, and he faced another hurdle. Doctors had given up on his being able to breathe without a respirator. In November, though, he said, "I want to try this again." With his first attempt he averaged 80 cubic centimeters (cc) of air per breath, "which wouldn't keep a parakeet alive," Reeve said. "The next day my motivation was very strong, and I was able to average 450 cc per breath. The doctors were stunned." The day after, he took 560 cc of air, and the following day, he told the doctors to take him off the ventilator. "Let me see how long I can breathe," he said. Reeve breathed on his own for seven and a half minutes. "I was sucking for air, my eyes were going up in my head, but eventually I breathed on my own."

A man of Reeve's size would require 1,200 cc of air, but he was making progress. Soon he would be able to take in 860 cc—far more than the "parakeet" breaths he started with. For a man who once soared like an eagle, both as Superman and as a pilot, he had come a long way toward accep-

tance of his disability and toward a healthy appreciation of
the kinds of accomplishments he could now make. In the
months ahead, those accomplishments would turn into his-
toric milestones.

On August 26, 1996, Reeve addressed the Democratic National Convention in Chicago. He praised the American people for their willingness to attempt the impossible, but he also sternly warned the government not to "trash programs that people need."

9

LIFTING A NATION

President Roosevelt showed that a man who could barely lift himself
out of a wheelchair could lift this nation out of despair.
—Christopher Reeve, 1996 Democratic Convention

IT WAS NOT until December 13, 1995, that Reeve could leave Kessler for good. Arriving home, he drove his wheelchair up the newly built ramp by puffing air into a strawlike device. It was time to take up his life where he had left off, imprisoned, however, by his immobile body. Reeve's doctors had predicted that his homecoming would trigger depression. "But instead, it was a tremendous boost," Reeve said. The doctor, visiting after a few days, found him breathing better, his blood pressure, oxygen levels, and blood and protein counts up. Little Will's spirits soared, too; he had missed climbing into his father's lap.

At home, Reeve could breathe without his respirator for 15 minutes, and he stopped using a feeding tube. But he still could not feed himself, perspire, or control his bladder. He also had to be moved every three hours to keep his muscles and joints limber.

Dana became fully involved in her husband's care, but Reeve needed outside help in case his ventilator accidentally shut down. He insisted that he have nurses to help monitor him and to allow Dana time off so she could get back to her acting.

Reeve began 1996 by working at his rehabilitation and lobbying to find a cure for spinal-cord injuries. He told friends that by his 50th birthday he intended to stand up and raise his arm in a toast to his family for keeping him alive through his rehabilitation.

But first, he had to solve the more immediate problem of paying his $400,000 annual medical costs. Reeve's insurance policy had a lifetime cap of $1.2 million, and he was no longer wealthy. He therefore readily agreed to support Vermont senator James Jeffords's amendment to raise the lifetime insurance limit for catastrophic illnesses to $10 million. He wrote a letter to each senator in Washington, urging them to approve it.

In January, Random House Publishers offered Reeve a welcome $3 million advance for a book about his recovery. His personal financial worries allayed, he turned his attention to the larger issue of raising funds for research into repairing damaged nerve tissue. He encouraged his friend and fellow equestrian Joan Irvine Smith to establish a multi-million-dollar facility. The Reeve-Irvine Research Center at the University of California opened on January 10, 1996.

Six days later, Reeve was rushed to Northern Westchester Hospital Center with autonomic dysreflexia—an ever-present danger in paralysis—resulting from a urinary tract infection. (Autonomic dysreflexia can also result from bowel blockage.) Doctors stabilized him and he was able to go home on January 22.

By early February, Reeve could breathe off the respirator for 90 minutes, and 75 percent of the sensation in his left leg had returned. He soon decided to make another public appearance. On March 10, in Green Springs, Ohio, he christened an $18 million wing of the St. Francis Health Care Centre, a state-of-the-art treatment facility for patients with spinal-cord injuries (SCI). "You can do anything you think you can," he told a gathering of patients there. He also joined the board of the American Paralysis Association, which raises research funds.

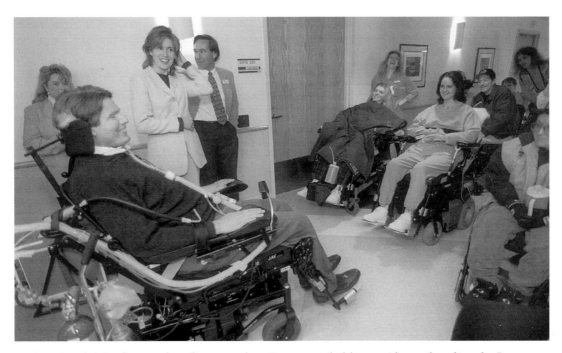

On March 25, after weeks of preparation, Reeve made his momentous appearance at the 68th Academy Awards in Los Angeles. "I felt so many warm and accepting faces," he told one reporter. "It felt like a homecoming."

Reeve's worries about his medical expenses eased as he accepted offers for paid speaking engagements scheduled for the rest of the year. By the first week of April, he was also cast as the voice of King Arthur in a Warner Bros. animated feature, *The Quest for Camelot.* On April 18, he addressed Peter Lowe's Success '96 Seminar, a motivational convention that has featured among its top speakers former First Lady Barbara Bush and Margaret Thatcher, the former prime minister of England.

In May he traveled once again to Washington, D.C., fighting for his cause. On the 13th he hosted a reception for the Dana Alliance for Brain Initiatives, a group raising funds for SCI research. The next day, he met with President Clinton, who pledged to allocate $10 million to the National Institutes of Health (NIH) for SCI research. Next Reeve appeared

After cofounding the Reeve-Irvine Research Center at the University of California in 1996, Reeve spent time that year visiting treatment facilities for patients with SCI and other disabilities. Here he talks with patients at Denver's Craig Rehabilitation Center.

before Congress with his friends—senators Paul Simon of Illinois, Pat Leahy of Vermont, Paul Wellstone of Minnesota, and John Kerry of Massachusetts—in the front row to support him.

That month, while Dana played Julia in the New Jersey Shakespeare Festival's *Two Gentlemen of Verona,* Reeve also reached a milestone in his own career: he took his place behind—rather than in front of—the camera as a film director. He met with producers Fred Zollo and Bonnie Timmermann, scriptwriter Will Scheffer, and HBO executives in his living room one day in May to discuss their upcoming project, an HBO television drama called *In the Gloaming,* about a young AIDS victim who returns to his parents' home to die. Despite Reeve's inexperience as a director, he challenged the team. "I said, 'I'm gonna open with a couple of comments that may get me fired here,'" he recalled. "I told them [the script] had potential, but it also had problems. It read like a play . . . [so] I said: 'Basic changes need to be made. If you think it's too much, by all means get somebody else. I'd be wrong for the movie.'"

But the team followed Reeve's advice. He called on the acclaimed stage and screen actress Glenn Close (*Fatal Attraction, 101 Dalmatians*) to play the mother. Close, a Bedford neighbor of Reeve's, sacrificed her vacation to take the part, saying she "really wanted to be with [Chris] in his first directing experience." Robert Sean Leonard (*Dead Poets Society*), who played the son, admitted he was "skeptical of first-time directors, because the job's much harder than people think," but that Reeve "commanded a respect few first-time directors have." Actress and comedienne Whoopi Goldberg (who had hosted the Academy Awards program in March) agreed to play a nurse in the film.

A writer who visited the set reported that Reeve "found his rhythm with the help of an extraordinarily supportive production team." "In turn," the report continued, "he is a demonstrative director, extraordinarily attuned to the tiniest modulation in his actors' line readings." Reeve even looked the part, sporting an embroidered sign that read "Christopher Reeve—Director," made by prop master Ann Miller and hung from the back of his wheelchair. Jonathan Demme, who, along with Steven Spielberg and *Superman*'s Richard Donner, sponsored Reeve's membership to the Directors Guild, visited him on the set. Demme greeted Reeve warmly with a kiss on the cheek.

Reeve continued to strive for physical improvements. By June he could breathe for several hours without his respirator. At the end of the month, he and Dana hosted a three-day Celebrity Sports Invitational in Dorado, Puerto Rico, which netted $300,000 for the American Paralysis Association. Robin Williams, who was an active presence at the event, told reporters, "I'd need a thesaurus to say everything I want to say about [Dana]. . . . She's living proof that angels don't all have wings." On June 28, the cabaret in Williamstown where Reeve and Dana met was dedicated to them, and Dana performed the song she sang when Chris first saw her. "It's one of the most touching things that's ever happened to Chris and me," Dana told a reporter. That month Reeve also announced to writer Liz Smith that Merchant Ivory Films wanted him to direct a movie for them and that the Williamstown Theatre Festival had asked him to direct a play.

In early July, Reeve agreed to play a small but important role in *A Step Toward Tomorrow*, a CBS movie about a mother whose insurance company refuses to pay for her paralyzed son's rehabilitation. Reeve's character counsels and inspires the family. Filming began that month. He also announced plans to narrate an HBO documentary, *Without Pity*, which would chronicle the lives of several disabled people.

In July Reeve also did something he never thought he could do again: he went sailing. On July 12, he was hoisted aboard the 12-meter *Northern Light* in his wheelchair and strapped to the boat's cockpit. He set sail with boat owners Elizabeth and Bob Tiedemann in a regatta in Narragansett Bay, off Newport, Rhode Island. Shake-a-Leg, a national group promoting rehabilitation and recreation for people with SCI, sponsored the three-day race. Famous sailors skippered the boats, and each yacht had a disabled crew member. Several hours into the race, tropical storm Bertha hit Newport, pouring down rain and buffeting the boats about. As they sailed through the rain a "magical" thing happened, Reeve later told the other sailors: the sound of the raindrops bouncing off his foul-weather gear drowned out the noise made by his ventilator. "I completely forgot that I'm in a chair," he said. Dana told Mrs. Teidemann it was the happiest she had seen her husband in over a year. "He had a smile on his face the entire time on the water," Tiedemann said.

Dana skippered the yacht part of the way, with winds blowing at 30 knots, and Reeve offered instructions as they went. Their boat finished second.

Hope for Reeve—and for all SCI victims—dawned into a glimmer of reality on July 26, when scientists announced that they had partially repaired the severed spinal cords of 22 paralyzed rats, enabling them to move their legs and take some halting steps. Lars Olson and H. Cheng of Sweden's Karolinska Institute grafted delicate strands of nerve fibers from other areas of the rats' bodies and fastened them to their spinal cords. The scientists enabled the transplanted nerve cells to grow by eliminating a particular protein produced by the myelin sheath—a protective covering on the spinal cord neurons—that inhibits new nerve cell growth. Over six weeks, the nerve fibers of treated rats grew about one-half inch down their spinal columns.

But Cheng and Olson cautioned against expecting immediate success in humans with their technique. Because they performed their delicate operations right after cutting the rats' spinal cords, they still do not know if the technique could work for people with old injuries. In fact, the surgery is still considered too dangerous to perform on humans because they might lose whatever nerve function they have left.

Cheng and Olson's spinal cord nerve regeneration is one of several approaches that scientists are working on to restore nerve function in humans. A North Carolina doctor has

Readers of Good Housekeeping *magazine joined forces with Reeve to convince Pennsylvania senator Arlen Specter (left) to pledge $40 million of the National Institute of Health's 1997 budget to SCI research. The magazine featured a letter urging more funding for SCI research, which readers could clip and send to Specter. Senator Tom Harkin of Iowa is on the right.*

used a substance called AP4 to increase electrical conductivity in neurons, allowing some patients to regain limited sensation, and in some cases, bowel and bladder control. But, according to Andrew Blight, a neurosurgeon at the University of North Carolina, more progress could be made. At present, he said, "We have just a few people doing research in a fairly modest way. If we threw the resources into this that we put into the moon shot, then we could make real progress."

Reeve's fans around the country urged Senator Arlen Specter, chair of the Senate subcommittee in charge of appropriating funds for medical research within the National Institutes of Health, to allocate $40 million for SCI research.

Good Housekeeping magazine included a coupon in an article on Reeve that readers could clip, fill out, and send to Specter. It was a letter to him citing Cheng and Olson's findings as a good reason to allocate money to SCI research. The letter also echoed an argument of Reeve's, which was that SCI primarily affects young people with long life spans, so a cure could save billions in government Medicare and Medicaid funds in the long run. Impressed by the groundswell of public support and by Reeve's lobbying efforts, Specter agreed to pledge $40 million of the 1997 NIH budget to SCI research.

Victory followed victory in Reeve's campaign to bring the plight—and the indomitable spirits—of the disabled to the public foreground. In the third week of August he emceed the Atlanta Paralympic Games, the Olympics for disabled athletes.

Reeve made another memorable appearance on August 26, 1996, at the Democratic Convention in Chicago, where delegates from around the country gathered to nominate President Bill Clinton as the party's candidate in the upcoming November election. Reeve personified the party's goal as stated by Connecticut senator Joseph Lieberman: "to empower people." He appeared last among a series of guests representing social issues the Democratic Party supported.

When Reeve's turn finally came, he was introduced as "an example of what one individual can do to move the world." Reeve, who was seated at the podium, smiled with pride and delight as the entire audience thundered an ovation. "I don't know that I deserve it," he said into the microphone. Television cameras panned to First Lady Hillary Clinton standing to applaud him, and to Dana, who stood at her side.

"Well I just have to start with a challenge to the president," Reeve quipped, "I've seen your train [on the president's whistle-stop campaign] go by and I think I can beat it." Reeve grinned mischievously as the audience broke into laughter. "I'll even give you a head start," he added.

He began his speech by defining family values, a central

theme of the campaign. "I think it means that we're all family . . . and that we all have value . . ." Cheers of approval burst from the crowd. Reeve went on, " . . . and that we have to recognize that many members are hurting," from "the neighbor with spinal cord injury" to "the brother with AIDS. We have got to do something about it. Our nation cannot tolerate disability of any kind." The crowd cheered more. Reeve advocated the Americans with Disabilities Act, describing it as a law that is "breaking down barriers," not only to buildings, but to "every opportunity in society."

His face hardened into a deadly serious expression, his brow furrowing, his eyes boring into the crowd, the cameras. "We have got to take care of our family and not trash programs that people need." He went on to call for more research to find cures for disabilities. "To do this we don't need to raise taxes, we just need to raise our expectations," he said, adding, "America has a tradition that many nations envy. We frequently achieve the impossible. That's part of our national character."

He then described a photograph that hung on the wall of his hospital room after his accident: a shot of the space shuttle blasting off, autographed by astronauts at NASA, which read, "We found nothing is impossible." "Now that should be our motto," Reeve said, grinning with pride. "So many dreams at first seem impossible and then seem improbable and then, when we summon the will, they soon become the inevitable. Still, if we can go to outer space, we should be able to conquer inner space, too . . . the frontier of the brain, the central nervous system and all the afflictions of the body that destroy . . . human lives."

Reeve enlarged his perspective to place the issue within a historical context, going back 56 years to Democratic president Franklin Delano Roosevelt (FDR), who was wheelchair-bound by polio. "President Roosevelt showed that a man who could barely lift himself out of a wheelchair could lift this nation out of despair," Reeve said, alluding to FDR's economic programs to put jobless Americans to work during

Reeve rehearses his speech for the 1996 Democratic National Convention with program producer Gary Smith (left). The actor put his powerful presence to good use at the convention, making a compelling case for government programs for the disabled.

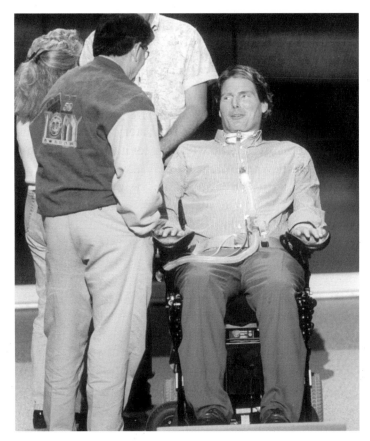

the Great Depression in the 1930s and to his leadership during World War II. "The most important principle that FDR taught us," Reeve said, "is that America does not let its needy citizens fend for themselves." The crowd roared in agreement. Cameras focused on tearstained faces, moved both by Reeve's condition and by his impassioned words. "America is strong when all of us take care of all of us," Reeve said in closing. "Giving new life to that ideal is the challenge before us tonight." He thanked his listeners. Cameras turned to Dana, elegantly dressed with upswept hair, her face wet with tears, as she stood smiling and applauding her husband. Reeve was wheeled offstage and President Clinton, live from Ohio, appeared on a huge screen to thank Reeve and to reiterate his message.

Bill Clinton went on to defeat the Republican candidate, Senator Bob Dole of Kansas, on November 5.

Reeve spoke out publicly again in the name of the handicapped when *Without Pity: A Film About Abilities* aired on HBO on October 8. He narrated the individual stories of people with cerebral palsy, blindness, polio, and SCI.

The most telling profile was the story of Josh, a young man from DeSoto, Texas, with SCI, for it described some of the personal anguish Reeve himself may have suffered privately. "I have to put on a facade for people, because if I were to let all the anger inside me out all the time, no one would want to be around me," Josh said. The film showed Josh's sister tirelessly caring for him, checking his urine bag to prevent infection and taking him to the toilet every night in a chair. "Having to ask people to do this for you is devastating," Josh said. "He's irritable a lot," Reeve commented. "He wears on everyone." Josh was suicidal. But "determination" comes "for some," Reeve said.

By the end of the film, Josh was shown completing his college degree in environmental engineering. "Disabled people want most to have independence," Reeve said in closing. "Many are forced to live in poverty. . . . [They] feel segregated from [society]. . . . tired of being invisible, they want to be understood for their humanity, without pity."

On November 10, *A Step Toward Tomorrow* aired on CBS. It was hailed as a celebration of the human spirit.

Reeve continued to appear throughout the country, inspiring people to support the SCI cause and motivating other SCI victims to persevere as he had. On January 12, 1997, he went home to the place where he began his career, Princeton's McCarter Theatre. Carly Simon, Mandy Patinkin, John Lithgow, and other friends performed at a concert to raise funds for SCI research, with Reeve as the guest of honor.

Reeve's campaign to find a cure for SCI continues. Arthur Ullian, who first prompted him to take up the cause, credits Reeve with successfully bringing the plight of SCI victims home to Americans. "You'd never have got the national fo-

Christopher and Dana Reeve enjoy a standing ovation at Princeton's McCarter Theatre in 1997. Reeve was the guest of honor at a fund-raising concert for the newly formed Christopher Reeve Foundation, which sponsors research to develop a cure for SCI.

cus without him," he said. "You'd never have got the excitement at NIH. Unfortunately, diseases need icons. Reeve has been that." Reeve himself has said, "The stage has been set. Awareness of spinal cord injury is at an all-time high. People now understand that something that was thought incurable can be cured. The politicians are motivated, the scientists are motivated, the public is showing concern, and everything is prepared to push to a successful conclusion."

Despite Reeve's fierce determination to be cured, his efforts may aid future SCI victims more than himself. "Walk-

ing is not the be-all and end-all for spinal-cord injury," Dr. Wise Young of NYU has said. "Independence is." Barring that, Reeve has shown the world what it is to be a hero.

Paradoxically, it has meant being able to accept the love and caretaking of others, as well as persevering with his own rehabilitation and leading as a fund-raiser, educator, and motivator. His life as he knew it—skippering a sailboat, piloting a plane, skiing down nearly vertical alpine slopes, and standing center stage—has been taken away. The dream of flight only lingers in his memory. Now trapped within a wooden body, Reeve has created a new and no less vital life for himself. Relying on his tireless will to win, he has emerged a more powerful fighter than he was when facing down the Pinochet regime in Chile. No matter what the outcome of his struggle, Reeve will remain a role model for people striving to overcome any handicap, offering an example of courage, perseverence, and endurance.

Good Housekeeping magazine listed Reeve 4th among the top 10 "Men We Admire Most" in its January 1997 issue because, as his citation read, "Instead of letting tragedy turn him into a martyr, he became a true crusader." Reeve ranked just behind the Reverend Billy Graham, Bill Clinton, and former president Jimmy Carter. In a touching testimony to Dana's unwavering love and care, the magazine listed her 8th among its 10 "Women We Admire Most" saying, "She exemplifies what marriage vows should mean. Her loyalty, courage, and love are absolutely outstanding." *People* magazine featured Reeve among the "25 most intriguing people" of 1996, noting that he did not let "catastrophe turn his wheelchair into a prison." He made it, instead, "his seat of power."

Despite what some have said, Reeve doesn't believe his accident happened for a reason. "It was an accident, it just happened," he says. "But now I have the opportunity to make sense out of it. I believe it's what you do *after* a disaster that gives it meaning," he adds.

With what he has made of his tragedy, Christopher Reeve has lifted a nation.

CHRONOLOGY

1952	Born on September 25 in New York City
1956	Moves with mother, Barbara Pitney Lamb Reeve, and brother, Benjamin, to Princeton, New Jersey
1959	Barbara marries investment banker Tristan Johnson in Princeton
1962	Takes to the stage in his first performance, singing in the McCarter Theatre production of Gilbert and Sullivan's *The Yeoman of the Guard*
1968	Becomes an apprentice at the Williamstown Theatre Festival, beginning a lifelong relationship with the Williamstown Theatre
1969	First major performance, as Beliaev in Turgenev's *A Month in the Country* at the Loeb Drama Center in Cambridge, Massachusetts; also performs at Maine's Boothbay Playhouse and at the San Diego Shakespeare Festival
1970	Enters Cornell University in Ithaca, New York
1973	Selected to attend New York's Juilliard School for drama instruction
1974	Graduates Cornell with a B.A. in English and music
1974–76	Plays Ben Harper on TV soap opera *Love of Life*
1975	Lands first Broadway role, as Nicky in *A Matter of Gravity* opposite Katharine Hepburn
1976	Makes film debut in *Gray Lady Down*
1977	Wins role of Superman in the Alexander and Ilya Salkind movie
1978	Falls in love with British model Gae Exton; *Superman, the Movie* becomes a box-office hit
1979	Given British Academy's Best Actor Award; stars in *Somewhere in Time*
1980	Stars in *Superman II;* Exton gives birth to Matthew Reeve; performs in *The Cherry Orchard, The Front Page,* and *The Heiress* at Williamstown; plays lead role in *The Fifth of July*
1981	Plays Achilles in *The Greeks* at Williamstown; named one of Ten Outstanding Young Americans by the United States Jaycees
1982	Costars with Michael Caine in the film *Deathtrap;* plays Father Flaherty in *Monsignor* and receives negative reviews
1983	Costars with Richard Pryor in *Superman III*

1984	Costars with Vanessa Redgrave in Merchant and Ivory's film adaptation of Henry James's *The Bostonians;* costars in Redgrave's stage revival of James's *The Aspern Papers;* receives Circle K Humanitarian Award; Exton gives birth to Alexandra Reeve
1985	Costars with Jacqueline Bisset in his first TV movie, *Anna Karenina;* stars in *The Royal Family* at Williamstown; plays Count Almaviva in *The Marriage of Figaro* in New York
1986	Campaigns for Vermont Senator Patrick Leahy on environmental issues
1987	Plays Jonathan Fisher in the film *Street Smart;* cowrites and stars in *Superman IV: The Quest for Peace;* breaks off relationship with Exton; meets and falls in love with Dana Morosini at Williamstown; travels to Chile to speak out against the Pinochet regime
1988	Receives two awards for his bravery in Chile from The Walter Briehl Human Rights Foundation; plays Blaine Bingham in the film *Switching Channels;* plays opposite Christine Lahti in the play *Summer and Smoke* in Los Angeles; plays Major John Dodge in the TV movie *The Great Escape II*
1989	Plays Polixenes opposite Mandy Patinkin in Joe Papp's production of *The Winter's Tale;* plays dual role in *John Brown's Body* at Williamstown
1990	Narrates TV documentary *Black Tide;* lobbies in Washington for Clean Air Act; tours nationally in *Love Letters;* tours the country to raise funds for AIDS victims; co-founds the Creative Coalition; lobbies in Washington to protect the National Endowment for the Arts (NEA)
1991	Costars with Meredith Baxter in TV movie *Bump in the Night*
1992	Marries Dana Morosini; costars in four TV movies: *Death Dreams, The Last Ferry Home, Mortal Sins, Nightmare in Daylight;* costars with Michael Caine and Carol Burnett in the film *Noises Off*
1993	Plays Senator Lewis in Merchant Ivory's *The Remains of the Day*
1994	Appears in the film *Speechless;* narrates a PBS documentary on gray whales
1995	Plays town doctor Alan Chaffee in the film *Village of the Damned;* travels to Arizona with Creative Coalition to fight censorship; plays a paralyzed police officer in the HBO movie *Above Suspicion;* falls in an equestrian competition in Virginia and becomes quadriplegic; undergoes surgery to reconnect his spine and skull; begins intensive rehabilitation; attends benefit dinner for Robin Williams; leaves Kessler Rehabilitation Center to go home in December

1996   Appears at 68th Academy Awards ceremony in Los Angeles; cast as voice of King Arthur in animated feature *Quest for Camelot;* campaigns in Washington for spinal-cord injury (SCI) research funding; takes on first film directing job with *In the Gloaming;* gives motivational speeches throughout the country; hosts the Paralympics in Atlanta; appears in TV movie *A Step toward Tomorrow;* narrates *Without Pity* for HBO; speaks at the Democratic National Convention in Chicago

1997   Ranked 4th on *Good Housekeeping* magazine's list of 10 "Men We Admire Most"

FURTHER READING

Bandler, Michael. "It Isn't Easy Being Superman." *McCalls,* September 1987, 53–54.

Begley, Sharon. "To Stand and Raise a Glass." *Newsweek,* 1 July 1996, 52–56.

Cerio, Gregory, et al. "Fallen Rider." *People,* 12 June 1995, 92–98.

Daly, Steve. "A New Direction." *Entertainment Weekly,* 15 November 1996, 32–37.

"Friends, Indeed." *People,* 30 October 1995: 56–58.

Green, Michelle. "He Will Not Be Broken." *People,* 15 April 1996, 116–125.

Hall, Adrian. *Man of Steel.* New York: Signet, 1996.

Harmetz, Aljean. "On Location with Christopher Reeve." *New York Times,* 6 July 1979, 65.

Kael, Pauline. "The Woman Question." *The New Yorker,* 6 August 1984, 68.

Kroll, Jack. "Superman to the Rescue." *Newsweek,* 1 January 1979, 46–51.

Matthiessen, Sarah. "Christopher Reeve after *Superman.*" *After Dark,* October 1980, 48–51.

Moritz, Charles, ed. *The Current Biography Yearbook.* New York: H. Wilson, 1982.

Park, Jeannie, and Vicki Sheff-Cahan. "Eat Your Heart Out, Lois." *People,* 20 April 1992, 141–143.

Petrou, David Michael. *The Making of Superman, the Movie.* New York: Warner Bros., 1978.

Rosenblatt, Roger. "New Hopes, New Dreams." *Time,* 26 August 1996, 40–52.

Rosenblatt, Roger. Biography of Christopher Reeve. New York: Random House, forthcoming.

Smith, Liz. "We Draw Strength from Each Other." *Good Housekeeping,* June 1996, 86.

"The Will to Live." *People,* 26 June 1995, 55–56.

INDEX

PICTURE CREDITS

Margaret L. Finn, a native of Philadelphia, holds a B.A. in sociology from the University of Pennsylvania and an M.A. in English from Beaver College, where she also taught freshman composition. She has produced an alumni magazine for the Wharton Graduate School of Business of the University of Pennsylvania, and she is fiction editor of the literary journal *Northeast Corridor.* Ms. Finn has also written *Mary Tyler Moore* for Chelsea House.

Jerry Lewis is the national chairman of the Muscular Dystrophy Association (MDA) and host of the MDA Labor Day Telethon. An internationally acclaimed comedian, Lewis began his entertainment career in New York and then performed in a comedy team with singer and actor Dean Martin from 1946 to 1956. Lewis has appeared in many films—including *The Delicate Delinquent, Rock-a-Bye Baby, The Bellboy, Cinderfella, The Nutty Professor, The Disorderly Orderly,* and *The King of Comedy*—and his comedy performances, such as his 1995 role in the Broadway play *Damn Yankees,* continue to delight audiences around the world.

John Callahan is a nationally syndicated cartoonist and the author of an illustrated autobiography, *Don't Worry, He Won't Get Far on Foot.* He has also produced three cartoon collections: *Do Not Disturb Any Further, Digesting the Child Within,* and *Do What He Says! He's Crazy!!!* He has recently been the subject of feature articles in the *New York Times Magazine,* the *Los Angeles Times Magazine,* and the *Cleveland Plain Dealer,* and has been profiled on *60 Minutes.* Callahan resides in Portland, Oregon.

--
B
Reeve
F

Finn, Margaret L.

Christopher Reeve.

8.95

DATE			